Deep and profound trust between human beings, especially now, is nothing less than sacred. In fact, I believe it's the currency that a truly spiritual life depends on. For God—or whatever name we use to define that which is most sacred—to enter into this world through us, we must learn how to be deeply trustworthy.

– Andrew Cohen, March 2009

AMERICAN GURU

A Story of Love, Betrayal and Healing—
former students of Andrew Cohen speak out

WILLIAM YENNER *and contributors*

www.americanguru.net

EPIGRAPH BOOKS
RHINEBECK, NEW YORK

Author contact: americanguru@ymail.com

Cover design by Peter Kitchell
Book design by Georgia Dent
Printed in the United States of America

Library of Congress Control Number: 2009932216
ISBN: 9780982453056

Epigraph Books
An Alternative Publishing Imprint of
Monkfish Book Publishing Company
27 Lamoree Road
Rhinebeck, New York 12572
www.epigraphPS.com
USA 845-876-4861

CONTENTS

ACKNOWLEDGMENTS

I AM GRATEFUL to the *What Enlightenment?!!* blog (whatenlighten-ment.net) and its editors, Hal Blacker and Stas Mavrides. Its many informative posts from former students of Andrew Cohen have been an invaluable reference in the completion of this book. I want to thank my editor, Kelly Horan, for all her hard work. I appreciate the patience and support of my wife, Sasha, and her willingness to hang in there through many long discussions and deliberations. And finally, my deepest thanks to all of the wonderful friends who have shared this journey with me, whose willingness to explore our individual and collective experiences has generated so much depth and insight.

FOREWORD

I first met Andrew Cohen in the autumn of 1985. He stayed for a few days in the Sharpham North Community near Totnes in Devon, England, to which I belonged at the time. I remember him as a rather intense and voluble young man. Shortly afterwards he left for India to participate in a vipassana retreat in Bodh Gaya.

About six months later, a friend returned from India and told me in hushed, ecstatic tones that Andrew had become enlightened upon meeting an Indian guru called Poonja-ji in Lucknow. I was surprised: I had no idea of what to make of the information. Over the next weeks, a trickle of people arrived in Totnes, all bearing the same good news. Many of them had just spent time around Andrew in Rishikesh. They were convinced that something extraordinary was happening. Then Alka, Andrew's girlfriend, arrived in Devon and joined the staff at Gaia House, a nearby retreat centre, where I was starting to teach. I listened to her recount the same story again and again. She was calm, collected and focused yet fired with a passionate conviction that a great guru, a world teacher comparable to the Buddha, had appeared. As much as I liked and respected Alka, I was skeptical.

Andrew returned to Devon, his way having been well prepared by those who preceded him. The anticipation and curiosity about him had reached a fever pitch by then. He started holding *satsang,* or teaching, in a small house in the village of Ashprington, near Sharpham. The meetings were soon packed. Andrew and his followers moved to a larger venue in Beenleigh, a nearby farm. One by one, my fellow community members and other friends in the area went to hear Andrew. Almost without exception, they were overwhelmed by the extraordinary effect Andrew's teaching and presence had upon them.

I was reluctant to go. This may have had to do with my own insecurity as a young Buddhist teacher. I did not want my convictions to be undermined by someone who, despite all the claims made about him, still struck me as immature. Nor had I ever had much time for Advaita Vedanta and Indian mysticism in general, which I found over-emotional and intellectually incoherent. But, I had to admit, perhaps this was just my Buddhist prejudice against Hinduism. So one evening I went to the *satsang* at Beenleigh to see what the fuss was about.

I squeezed into a poorly lit room, packed with people, many of whom I knew, sitting in silence, eyes closed, cross-legged on the floor. Then Andrew appeared, radiant and smiling, and sat on an old armchair in one corner. It was one of the most tedious evenings I can remember.

My strongest impression was one of massive transference and counter-transference — these were psychoanalytic terms I recall using at the time to best describe what I witnessed. Much of the evening was spent in silence, punctuated by a phrase or comment from Andrew, then, toward the end, a number of exchanges between him and some of the students. Andrew said nothing that was remotely memorable: it was blend of mystical Hindu-Buddhist platitudes of the sort found in many popular tomes on Eastern philosophy and religion. But the audience was entranced. Often after Andrew made some remark, you would hear an orgasmic gasp from someone in the room as though they had just been shown the face of God.

What was going on here clearly had little if anything to do with what Andrew was saying. The "teaching" and "dialogue" were merely devices for building and sustaining an emotional bond between Andrew and the students. While the students experienced some sort of ecstasy by collectively projecting their spiritual longings and ideals onto Andrew, Andrew seemed to need the adulation of others to endorse the sense of being the enlightened guru he and his students wanted him to be. The more this interchange of mutually reinforcing desires went on, the greater became the certainty that Andrew really was the savior of our age and the students his first blessed circle of disciples. As long as this bubble of shared conviction remained intact, everyone got what they wanted.

I found it bewildering that so many of my friends were sucked into this solipsistic whirlpool. The Sharpham community emptied out until only my wife and I and one other person were left. The committee that ran Gaia House dwindled to almost nothing as trustees resigned in order to follow Andrew. People I thought I knew well ignored me. Being outside their charmed circle, it was as though I were invisible. I would find myself in the same room as a group of shiny-eyed "Androids" but was excluded as they ranted on about their sole obsession: Andrew Cohen. For them, I was just another benighted soul who was unable to "open" to what Andrew was saying. I confess that there were moments when I had the terrifying doubt that rather than being the only sane person in a community gone mad, perhaps I was the last surviving madman in a community gone sane.

Then, to my relief, Andrew and his followers decided to go to America. I saw Andrew only once again, when he briefly returned to Devon a year or two later. I went to another *satsang,* but found it just as incomprehensible as the time before.

The only way I can describe what I witnessed in Devon in the 1980s was the formation of a cult: a closed system of millenarian belief exclusively focused on a single person who claimed absolute authority. I regret now not having spoken out more strongly against what was going on around Andrew Cohen at the time. But not only was I confused and uncertain myself, it was impossible to have a rational conversation with anyone who had chosen to follow Andrew. For what could an unenlightened intellectual like me possibly have to say about a teacher whose every word is an expression of his unconditional relationship with the Absolute?

Authoritarian religion is one of the greatest dangers facing humankind in our world today. Whether that authoritarianism be Christian, Muslim, Hindu or Buddhist makes no difference. In each case, an elite group claims absolute authority on the basis of a text or a mystical revelation, then seeks to impose that authority on others as the only way to achieve personal and collective salvation. In this way, imperfect humans will be rendered more perfect until the day comes when a heaven on earth is realized. Yet no matter how often we observe such fantasies inflict enormous human suffering, our appetite for more seems undiminished. This is curious. Even intelligent and educated people remain vulnerable to the *ex cathedra* promises of messiahs. It is as though a core part of ourselves has never really grown up. Rather than take responsibility for our own lives, we willingly hand it over to someone else who claims to have direct access to God or the Absolute.

"I do not *deny* that we may have 'experience of God,'" wrote the English Buddhist monk Nanavira Thera in 1965. "Numinous experience is just as real as sex or romantic love or aesthetic experience; and the question that must be answered is whether these things are to be taken at face value as evidence of some kind of transcendent reality or whether the eternity they point to is a delusion." All belief in an unconditioned reality that transcends the contingent, painful flux of this world is, I suspect, an understandable but dangerous delusion. Rather than directing our longing and energy towards the Absolute and the spiritual freedom it promises, we need to turn our attention back to this world with all its messiness and suffering. For if there is any liberation to be found, it will be found here, in the midst of ordinary life, as a freedom from the grasping and craving for the self or the world to be perfect.

Stephen Batchelor
Aquitaine, March 2009

INTRODUCTION

N
o one knowingly joins a cult. I spent more than thirteen years following the American guru Andrew Cohen. It was a time that began in love and beauty, a time during which I forged many of my closest friendships and found deep spiritual meaning. I became a leader in Andrew's community and felt energized and fulfilled by the work I did on his behalf. For many years, my discipleship to Andrew gave my life purpose, satisfaction and hope. Eventually, however, darkness clouded the light that had illuminated the first years of my association with Andrew Cohen. What had been my choice at the outset — to abandon life as I knew it to follow a charismatic guru — gradually came to feel less like a life freely chosen than forced enlistment in the service of an individual bent on total control.

Initially, Andrew Cohen seemed to many of us to embody perfection. Upon meeting him, I questioned everything. I left my home and my marriage and moved into a group home in Boston, where I shared a bedroom with two other men. Privacy meant little with the prospect of enlightenment at hand, and for many years that prospect sustained my fellow students and myself, fostering a deep love and trust that flourished among us. Many of the friendships I forged then remain strong to this day — and some have grown in depth — despite the fact that ninety-five percent of those of us who were original members have left the community.

When I left Andrew's community, and for many years after, anger and blame dominated my emotions. I was nearly consumed by a paralyzing resentment. The notion that I might ever be able to forgive Andrew was inconceivable to me. What I didn't realize at the time was that I first had to forgive myself. That realization came to me as silently as melting snow, and it startled me. Forgiveness is essential to healing, and forgiving myself — for the years that I devoted to Andrew and his organization, for the role I played in it, for my complicity in the abuses that occurred there —

has gradually opened me to the possibility that I might one day forgive Andrew. I am not completely there — this is a process that may take a lifetime — but even my acceptance of it as a possibility I regard as progress.

Working toward forgiveness rather than stewing in indignation and resentment has allowed me to size up my experiences as Andrew's disciple, and to present my memories fairly and in their proper context. The benefit of hindsight has served me in the writing and assembling of the essays presented here, tempering my resentment and informing my understanding of the process through which the community I left had become so different from the one I'd entered. I present this book in order to set the record straight, to withdraw my thirteen-year endorsement of my former guru, and to shed light on Andrew Cohen and his organization for the sake of anyone previously, currently or prospectively involved with him.

I am joined in these pages by several contributors, all of whom are Andrew's former students. This is a testament to the spirit of communion that we have shared and continue to share in these, our "post-Andrew," years. Our collective goal is transparency: to examine, to describe and to better understand our experiences as individuals and as members of a devoted group of Andrew Cohen's followers. Ours is a story of the dark side of the quest for enlightenment, and of the disappointment we experienced when the person who had inspired us dashed our hopes and our spirits. Yet as a collection of individual reflections, observations and experiences, our story most emphatically does not represent a single point of view, nor is it told in a single voice; our perspectives and opinions differ, and this project is richer for it.

The complexity inherent in the guru/disciple relationship has also inspired a broader exploration of authoritarian leadership and the enlightenment paradigm as a whole, and in the chapters that follow, contributors seek to answer such questions as:

- What inspires an individual to follow a guru?
- What makes an individual susceptible to the allure of an authoritarian teacher?

- What are the psychological needs of the spiritual seeker?
- What is the nature of enlightenment, and is devotion to a guru the surest way to attain it?
- What limitations inherent in the guru/disciple power dynamic might hinder transcendence?
- What comes after the guru if one still yearns for enlightenment?

Finally, this book is about healing. But for healing to take place, the silence must first be broken. Hard truths must be told about what happened during my thirteen years as a disciple of Andrew Cohen. Yet as the reader will see, the truths told here are still being *denied* by Andrew Cohen—which is precisely why reports like this one are important. I have struggled and railed against my recollection of what happened; I've been furious, I've calmed down, and now I write. I write, as previously stated, for the sake of the truth, for my own healing and that of others formerly or presently involved with an authoritarian guru. And I write, as well, for those seeking a more general insight into the powerful but potentially dangerous phenomenon of guru involvement.

In the minds of many, such experiences are best left alone, and one would do better to "move on with one's life." But the unfortunate truth is that a fracture occurs in the heart and mind when one's deepest love and trust in others is shattered—and "moving on," in and of itself, does nothing to restore that trust. For a time it may be necessary to disregard painful memories while reestablishing some semblance of normalcy and balance, renewing connections with work, other people and daily activities. My own view, though—and that of countless others I've consulted with—is that the silence must be broken. We each have our own way of doing this, and for me this book an important aspect of my own version of "breaking the silence." Ultimately, I believe, to remain silent about abuse is to enable the abuser, which can lead in turn to further harm to others.

Yet just as there is a great need for the truth to be spoken, it is also evident that it should not be forced or premature. In some cases, I have made the mistake of pushing too hard or too quickly in the process of this unveiling. It is retraumatizing to revisit old wounds, especially if one is not yet ready. Each must decide when and in what form to revisit these wounds and examine them; but when the light of truth is finally brought to bear, something begins to heal, some part of the trust that was lost is rediscovered, and a positive and empowering path opens—one that fosters the conditions necessary for healing and forgiveness, shows the way forward, and instills confidence that one is enriched by painful experiences if ultimately they serve to advance one's understanding.

In this act of healing I am also opening to all who have been my companions in the spiritual community that we built, along with its founder and leader, Andrew Cohen. Each of these people has given of himself or herself in an ultimate way, and shared that gift with me. Those who have remained close friends, as well as those who have vexed and challenged me—even rejected my way of dealing with these matters—have all been part of this defining experience. To all I am grateful, and I hope that this book will contribute something to everyone, even in disagreement. I understand that it may also stir controversy, that no one is likely to agree with all of it, and that many will take categorical exception to it. Therefore I wish to make it clear that it is not my desire to articulate an understanding that is universally acceptable; and that, as for my fellow contributors as for myself, we are each simply expressing our own view.

In order to avoid possible embarrassment to private individuals who figure in the incidents described, I have used pseudonyms in cases where permission to reveal their true identities could not be arranged. At the same time, the presence of anyone's name or story in this book is not meant to imply their endorsement of any of the statements made in it, as my goal is merely the opening of a conversation intended to result in deeper understanding.

William Yenner
July 2009

1

THE PRESENT

I feel obliged to preface this chapter with a warning that it expresses strong emotions. One reason why giving expression to these emotions is an important part of this process, both for myself and for the reader, is that *many* aspects of this story are simply difficult to believe. Particularly for someone familiar with Andrew Cohen's public presentation of himself, accepting what is revealed here requires a willingness to experience extreme feelings and responses, if only because the two pictures are so different that one could be forgiven for wondering who—if anyone—is really telling the truth. And it turns out that in situations like this, the raw emotion of anger serves as a useful and necessary conduit for recollection, incredulity and, ultimately, discernment.

"I remember," narrates Kyrsten Perry on a recent EnlightenNext webcast,

> [that] as soon as Andrew came into the room and sat down and started speaking, I was very aware that I was in the presence of a human being that had integrity. If someone is walking their talk, that has to be proven in time, but I intuited in my first meeting with him that he had a deep, fundamental human integrity. That was the first thing that struck me about him. The other thing was [that] I could see in him what is *the most possible thing* in our human incarnation. In our human incarnation there is the potential for so much more than we usually allow ourselves to contemplate, and he was expressing that in a very clear way. I've know him for about fourteen years now, and he's always expressed that.[1]

Especially at this late date in the unfolding of Andrew Cohen's "career," I am frankly angered to hear a current leader in his community describe him—in a posting on his official website—as the

---
1 "Our Experiment to Create a New Unity in Consciousness and Culture—The Inside Story of EnlightenNext's Evolution," posted April 24, 2009 (UK archive), enlightennext. org/webcast

rarest embodiment of what is possible for a human being. Yet I can also attest to the attraction of this message, as it is precisely what moved me, some twenty years ago, to join that community. On Cohen's website, andrewcohen.org, one learns the following:

> Spiritual mentor to hundreds of students worldwide, Cohen founded EnlightenNext in 1988, a nonprofit educational and spiritual organization dedicated to pushing the edge of progressive culture. In addition to an expanding network of individuals and groups around the world, EnlightenNext has public centers in New York, Boston, London, Amsterdam, Paris, Frankfurt, Copenhagen, and Rishikesh, India. The main center for EnlightenNext is a 220-acre retreat venue in western Massachusetts, where Cohen and his largest body of students currently reside.

What is presented here certainly sounds like a noble and well-motivated success story, and again, I can attest to its compelling attractiveness to the eyes, ears, mind and heart of an idealistic seeker. An active evolutionary mission around the world, fueled by a bold visionary's embodiment of the highest human potential—to idealistically predisposed individuals, which most spiritual seekers are, these represent a potentially irresistible combination. For some, of course, in order to understand the attraction, it may be necessary to set aside natural skepticism about the possibility of Cohen's prospectus being conceptually valid or realizable, but for others, it may simply strike them as "what they have been looking for." And it should be apparent that for those of us who have responded favorably, and who have given over a significant portion of our lives to participating in Andrew Cohen's "revolution," the act of fundamentally questioning the validity of the whole enterprise can be as disturbing as it clearly must be to Cohen himself.

While in the context of community life this process of questioning is one that occurs only in the most private and unacknowledged recesses of the student's mind, it nevertheless puts Cohen in the position of constantly having to reify his mission and its ever-evolving philosophical foundations—not only to his students, but to the readers of his publications, and to the other public figures in the alternative spirituality scene with whom he cultivates strategic alliances. All this "convincing" necessitates a calculated onslaught of public relations designed to fortify Cohen's audience—and perhaps even himself—against doubt. Under these conditions, the possibility that Andrew Cohen may be engaging in even a small fraction of the escapades to be described in this book becomes unavoidably disturbing to anyone who has grown to any degree accustomed to accepting his paradigm at face value.

Take this as a warning, then, that what follows may at times be charged with an energy that is strong or disturbing, and that if so, it's because it deals with the experience of two realities that couldn't be further apart, each competing for our attention and credulity. What is the truth? What I am going to describe in these pages, as hard as it may be to believe—and as angry as it makes me to unearth it—is actually the truth unadorned, and it is precisely because it *is* the truth, and precisely because Andrew Cohen *knows* it is the truth, that he consulted a lawyer to draw up a five-year gag order, and then persuaded me to sign it under conditions that he'd calculated would predispose me to do so.

What is the nature of the information that Andrew Cohen wanted to prevent me from making public? It is my own firsthand experience of operating, managing and leading his organization. For many years, I was a member of a small group of his closest students, an experience that eventually left me completely disillusioned with Cohen and his project, and from which it has taken me years to fully recover.

How does Andrew Cohen's use of a lawyer to silence me square with his professed ideals of enlightened understanding, transparency, and moral and ethical development? When one begins to look more deeply into this question, it becomes apparent that his whole enterprise is really just smoke and mirrors. I happen to have the goods on how he makes it all happen, and it is no coincidence that for the past five years I've been legally obligated to say nothing about it; now I'm sharing what I know for the benefit of anyone to whom it may prove helpful.

Over my years of service to Moksha Foundation—a.k.a. the Impersonal Enlightenment Fellowship, a.k.a. EnlightenNext—I witnessed the slow devolution of Andrew Cohen's "mission" first to spin, then to lies, and then to bigger and more elaborate lies. As strange as it sounds, my former teacher takes pride in (among other things) his ability to lie to and manipulate others. His community consists of concentric circles, each knowing only so much and not privy to what goes on in the ones above. Those who leave, declining at some point to participate in this game, are condemned, and it is Andrew's province alone to cast them definitively out of the circle with an explanation for their departure that he never tires of articulating: "They're *losers,* turning their backs on the holy life!"

It is important to understand that characterizations like this carry far more power than that of a single ordinary person's opinion, because of Andrew Cohen's ability to coordinate the opinions and actions of a large number of obedient students—at times even *against each other.* A telling anecdote is that of a longstanding current member of Cohen's community, a professional stage magician and "mentalist" named Gerard Senehi, who sometimes used to present his act on the streets of New York's Little Italy. Gerard had given his business card to a conspicuously well-dressed man who'd offered him a chance to perform at a private club "down the street" for some "friends of his," and was worried about the ethical implications of accepting money from figures possibly associated with organized crime. Armed with this information, Andrew gathered some spectators, swore them to secrecy and, impersonating a Mafioso, left a message on Gerard's voice mail specifying the date, time and location of the requested performance. He then arranged whenever possible to have other students listen in when Gerard called him from New York to discuss the ethics of performing for mobsters versus the possible dangers of declining or simply not showing up. (In the end, he chose the latter.)

As the prank escalated, Gerard received another message to the effect that, having turned down an opportunity to "make some money," he now was being given, for the last time, an "offer he couldn't refuse." It sounds like good fun if you are prepared to ignore the fact that Gerard (like many street performers) genuinely feared for his safety — a fact that Andrew skillfully justified to others as *karmic* retribution for the basis of Gerard's own livelihood, which was after all, he explained, trickery and deception. Yet Andrew's resentment of the attention Gerard received during the public performances he gave at EnlightenNext had not gone unnoticed, along with his tendency to somehow upstage Gerard, or put him in his place, near the end of each one. And it was also apparent that Andrew derived great pleasure from coordinating and executing this practical joke, especially with the support of an admiring and complicit audience.

I had the misfortune of being overheard by Gerard as I was describing the joke to a third party, giving the game away. The *karma* I had incurred by doing so, decreed my totally irritated guru, could only be erased by my own development of a scheme for toying with Gerard as effective as the one I had so carelessly ruined. Unbelievable as it is to me now, I put all my energy into fabricating a harshly worded demand letter to Gerard from a fictitious creditor — including a complete series of false documents on bank letterhead and stationery and a toll-free phone number for inquiries — about which he now had an entirely new set of desperately earnest ethical discussions with Andrew, who purported to be trying to help him with his latest problem.

Finally, before a gathering at the airport to see Andrew off on a teaching trip, an airport employee was paid ten dollars to deliver a mysterious envelope to Gerard, which Andrew insisted he open in front of everyone, containing the information that the letterhead was fake, the joke was on him, and that Andrew was the "real magician." As a result, he declared shortly thereafter, my *karma* was officially erased. Now, from the other side of the looking glass, I am astounded to recall how much my teacher *delighted* in events like this, and incredulous that I was so willing to be his accomplice. Yet there it is, and here we are.

Although by comparison with many of Cohen's excesses this is an incident that may seem relatively minor, it highlights the fundamental question of whether it is possible for an authentic spiritual teacher to derive *pleasure* from abuses of the power that his students give him over their lives and their destinies. Most of the acts of physical, emotional and financial abuse perpetrated by Cohen against his students are so shocking that, when they are actually described, people choose to believe either that they never happened or that, if they did, it was simply a matter of his having gone "a little too far." But while many of these acts, recounted in the pages that follow, are disturbing in themselves,[2] addressing the question of motivation is even more so — as is almost inevitably the case in situations involving those figures, such as parents and teachers, in whom we have placed our deepest trust. Was there *really* a "lesson" for Gerard in being treated this way? Or had Cohen orchestrated these events in such a way as to gratify — *while simultaneously deflecting attention from* — some malevolence, pleasure in deceit or lust for domination in himself? Is this the pathological template underlying Cohen's pervasive demonization and abuse of those students who dare to disobey, contradict or leave him?

In the process of reviewing my own experience, I have been compelled to admit that this is a greater possibility than I had ever allowed myself to imagine — making the present inquiry a very different sort of challenge than the one I thought I was signing on for as a student of "the truth." And with every page it becomes more apparent that I write what I write here not because I want to, but because Andrew Cohen has left me no choice. As the events recounted in this book reveal, Cohen's demonization of his students' "egoic tendencies" — tendencies which he himself has supposedly transcended — extend far beyond instructive spiritual "lessons," providing him with a pretext both for the administration of harsh

---

2 See in particular *Chapters 3, 4* and *7.*

discipline and punishment and the induction of soul-destroying intimidation and guilt. Aren't abusive or manipulative tendencies of this kind – rooted as they are in a desire for control – reflections of the very opposite of who and what, as an "enlightened" spiritual teacher, Cohen is supposed to represent? Perhaps it is not so surprising after all that formerly devoted students who, like myself, gave Andrew Cohen years of their lives, describe feeling confused, demoralized and upset – and not only by his treatment of them during their tenure as members of his community, but also by the coordinated vilification, within that community, that he has directed at them since their departures.

Far more pernicious than any practical joke, Cohen's wholesale demonization of his students is in fact a longstanding practice that predates by over a decade any criticism, public or private, to which they have individually or collectively subjected him,[3] and was for a long time so effective a guilt-inducing tactic that even those who left him remained silent. Slowly, however, this has been changing. In 1997, a book by Cohen's own mother, condemning his practices, was published,[4] followed by that of another former student, Andre Van der Braak.[5] By late 2004, so much pressure had been building over Andrew Cohen's suppression of disturbing information about life in his community that a blog by former students (whatenlightenment.net) began posting revealing accounts of serious abuse. Within months – true to form – that blog had been roundly condemned and ridiculed by Cohen and his representatives.

Among Cohen's most vocal defenders was Craig Hamilton, at that time the Managing Editor of Cohen's *What Is Enlightenment?* (now *EnlightenNext*) magazine – who subsequently left the community himself.[6] Articulating Cohen's customary explanation for

3 See *Chapter 3*.
4 See *Chapter 12*.
5 See *Chapter 7*.
6 This was the same individual who, in 1997, had paid a visit to the publisher of Van der Braak's book in order to discourage him, on Cohen's behalf, from releasing it. Its publication, he argued, would not be helpful to "the cause of the planet" – and the publisher, who was also a former student of Cohen's and thus "owed him his loyalty," would be sued if sufficient grounds for prosecution could be found. Finally, he communicated Cohen's desire to vet the book's contents prior to publication.

their uncooperative behavior, Hamilton wrote of these apostates
at the time:

> The "wisdom of the ego"...lies in its ingenious ability to distort real-
> ity to protect us from uncomfortable, even devastating truths. This is
> why authentic spiritual paths [i.e., Cohen's] are so challenging. They
> attempt to disarm the ego, so we can see clearly, free of its distortions.
> And as any tradition worth its salt will tell you, except in the rarest of
> cases, human beings will not give up their defenses without a fight.
> And most of the time, we won't give them up at all.[7]

It is a testament to the effectiveness of Cohen's airtight pro-
jections that he has never applied this logic to himself, always asserting that the truth-distorting "ego" is operative only in others.
As he insisted in his blog posting of October, 2006, "A Declaration
of Integrity,"[8] his own integrity was beyond question, while his
critics — too weak and selfish to face the truth about themselves —
were a "small number" of former students who had "failed" at
the spiritual life. And as he continued to speak around the globe
and to attract big names to his magazine — the Dalai Lama, Bishop
Desmond Tutu, Arianna Huffington, Robert F. Kennedy, Jr.,
and, of course, Ken Wilber — I and many other former students
found ourselves wondering how what was so real and evident to
us could remain so effectively hidden. Vexed by his unwilling-
ness — even in private — to engage in potentially healing dialogue
on the issues and concerns that his former students had brought
to his attention, I in particular longed for the opportunity to speak
openly that my former teacher had denied me.[9]

At the time of this writing, EnlightenNext is advertising a
twenty-day retreat scheduled for the summer of 2009 in Tuscany,

---

7 Craig Hamilton, "An Explosion of Liberation: Reflections of a Current Student," posted
February 4, 2005, as a comment on "A Legacy of Scorched Earth — Reflections of a Former
Student," whatenlightenment.net, February 2, 2005; see *Chapter 9*.
8 andrewcohen.org/blog, posted October 18, 2006
9 In 2005, Hal Blacker, former editor-in-chief of Cohen's *What Is Enlightenment?* magazine,
had written publicly on whatenlightenment.net: "Please come into this forum, Andrew.
Please be willing to truthfully admit your mistakes, and begin to help the process of truth
and reconciliation. It will be much better for everyone — you, your community, your former students, and your friends — if you participate with humility and honesty in this cer-
emony of healing and purification. Whether you participate or not, however, the truth will
come out. It must."

called "Being and Becoming," consisting of two ten-day retreats (the latter a networking conference), one for each topic. According to his video spokespeople on youtube.com and the enlighten-next.org website, what Cohen is offering at these retreats is an opportunity to "work with the creative energies of Evolutionary Enlightenment and…the creative potentials of the universe"; to find out "what it really takes and what it really means to evolve consciousness"; and to experience "something you won't find any-where else…an innovation from Andrew Cohen…an evolution-ary leap to a different potentiality between human beings…. For anyone who is interested in changing the world, it's this kind of energy that is actually going to lead to creating a new future."[10]

This is where twenty years of preaching truth and freedom have gotten EnlightenNext and Andrew Cohen: banal infomer-cials calculated to attract the most innocent and idealistic among us, while what happens behind closed doors — how he treats his subordinates and even those closest to him, his dismissive at-titudes toward women, the physical and mental abuses he en-gages in, and in which he encourages others to participate — are to remain shrouded in mystery. The possibility glimpsed by EnlightenNext student Michael Wombacher in *11 Days at the Edge*, an unquestioning account of his experiences at a previous retreat led by Cohen, is, unfortunately, a real one: "…[S]uddenly and without the slightest warning a black voice shot forth from some interior darkness, honed with the bloody edge of a guillotine. It proclaimed in a diabolical rage, 'He's crazy.'"[11]

But Wombacher's ultimate conclusion is part and parcel of the kind of spin that has enabled Cohen to retain and consolidate power over a new generation of submissive recruits:

> Thinking about this it was immediately obvious why some who had been deeply involved with Andrew and had, for one reason or an-other, parted from the teaching went to such extraordinary lengths to vilify him in as public and relentless a manner as possible. Such

---

10 "EnlightenNext Being & Becoming Retreat," youtube.com, posted May 1, 2009
11 Wombacher, Michael, *11 Days at the Edge: One Man's Journey into Evolutionary Enlighten-ment*, Forres, Scotland: Findhorn Press, 2008, p. 348

tactics were required for the individuals involved to make the case, first to themselves and then to others, that Andrew was a monster; then they could deny the monster in themselves.

The imagery employed here is Andrew Cohen's, not Wombacher's. As indicated above, likening the egos of his students to vampires, monsters and personifications of evil was and remains an habitual "teaching strategy" in the EnlightenNext community, one so graphic and common that one begins to suspect it is the projection outward of an "evil," feared and denied, that lies within. Cohen's apparent inability to engage in any respectful discussion with his former students, and his denial of any possibility that their grievances are legitimate or even real, perfectly exemplify the infuriating juxtaposition of two competing versions of reality that I am attempting to describe here.[12]

It seems that reducing the world to black and white—good and evil, "ego" and "authentic self"—carries for Andrew Cohen the added benefit of entitling him to say that black is white and white is black. In an attempt to squelch an article by Israeli journalist Yonatan Levy, Cohen had his "Communications Director," in collaboration with his lawyer, issue Levy a comprehensive denial of well-known events in his community that *dozens* of his students had witnessed or actually participated in—including the fact that he'd had me sign the above-mentioned contractual gag order![13] And yet it is supposedly his former students, whom he depicts as monsters, who are unable to "face themselves."[14]

---

12 Cohen's "Declaration of Integrity" concludes: "I was having a conversation with a respected philosopher and very dear friend one day several years ago, and I confided in him that some of my students who had left were turning against me. I remember being surprised and deeply moved when he replied, 'I know, Andrew. But they all know that you never lied to them.' And that's the bottom line."

13 See *Chapter 14*, Yonatan Levy's "interview" with EnlightenNext.

14 The lawyer mentioned above, from whom the journalist Levy received a threatening letter dated the same day as EnlightenNext's denials, is Barry A. Fisher, who, as reported in the *Washington Post* and the *Los Angeles Times*, traveled to Japan in 1995, to defend the Aum Shinrikyo cult against alleged government "persecution" following its lethal sarin gas attack on commuters in the Tokyo subway. Accompanying Fisher on this trip, which had been financed by Aum Shinrikyo, was James R. Lewis, director of the Association of World Academics for Religious Education—who in 1999, following a visit to EnlightenNext, contributed a laudatory preface to Andrew Cohen's book *In Defense of the Guru Principle*. (I was present during Lewis's visit, and had the opportunity to witness Cohen's displeasure—"Who does he think he is?"—upon receiving a bill for Lewis's hotel accommodations.) Additional information on Fisher and Lewis can be found on the Apologetics Research Resources website (apologeticsindex.org/a06ae.html).

There is another sort of monster, and the shock of recognizing it in one's own "enlightened" teacher is greater than that of
seeing for what they are the many egregious abuses he has perpetrated, more heartrending and demoralizing than the simple recognition of harm. It is the same shock that we experience when we
discover that our leaders have needlessly enmeshed themselves
in scandal, engaged in and covered up political dirty tricks, lied
to incite, justify or conceal a war, or detonated a nuclear weapon
as a show of strength. It is the shock of coming face to face with a
monster that destroys *because it can*, that derives an experience of
euphoria, arousal or pleasure from the recognition of what it can
get away with, believing that no one will stand in its way.

I remember Andrew saying many times, sometimes before
gatherings of a hundred or more devotees, "I don't care if I'm the
last one left—I'm *never* going to give up or change my position!"
The effect was always stunned silence. But this masquerade of
uncompromising spiritual integrity *worked;* we always remained
deeply deferential to him, and any open questioning was universally understood to be a mistake that would meet in the best case
with a harsh rebuke, while intensified "spiritual practice" or sum-
mary dismissal always hovered as threatening possibilities in the
background.

Do I believe that Andrew Cohen is an evil genius? No, nothing so monstrous or dramatic as that—although there is an obvious danger that his power over others amplifies his ability to
cause serious harm. In fact, as is often the case with well known
political figures who have wreaked havoc under the banner of
goodness, and who have justified their excesses with simplistic
and absolutized ideologies, Andrew Cohen's self-aggrandizing
hubris often strikes me less as diabolical than as childish and at
times even infantile. Understandably, though, none of us had the
courage or presence of mind to say after one of his tirades, "Hey
Andrew, you sound like a pissed off four-year-old!" He gets away
with it because for the most part his audiences, both intimate and
remote, are not inclined to believe that anyone could or would

lie so boldly and completely. So he carries on with his giant spin, representing himself as the sanest of human beings, with only the interests of others—and the evolution of the entire cosmos—at heart.

Many readers will doubtless wonder why so many of us put up with so much for so long. The answer is that, collectively, we fell under the sway of an ideology and a charismatic leader with a mission to match. I'm not embarrassed to admit this because something more important is at stake, namely the truth. And among many of us who have left EnlightenNext, there is a strong desire to stop walking on eggshells for the sake of those who remain. As I write this, it has been less than a month since the publication of documents that reveal Cohen's penchant for strategic dishonesty to be of the highest and most shameless order[15]; yet this has not prevented him from asserting only days ago, on his own blog, that the subtle evolutionary possibility he alone has envisioned for over twenty years "has now emerged and become stable between enough of us to make all the difference in the universe."[16]

As the chapters that follow reveal, neither Cohen's current nor his former students can be credibly accused of cynicism (no self-respecting cynic would ever dream of belonging to EnlightenNext); indeed, Cohen would never have been able to maintain a following in the first place if its members had not cognized for themselves the spiritual dimension of human experience—so what exactly is going on here? What he appears to be doing, perhaps quite compulsively, is capitalizing on the "subtlety" of spiritual experience as a way of explaining why some people remain loyal and receptive to him while others do not. "...Experienced as consciousness," he writes in the same self-redemptory blog post,

> [Spirit] is a higher and more subtle domain than our ordinary waking state. That's why it's so easy to temporarily awaken and see the face of God for oneself and then to not only lose access to that awareness but to even forget that it actually happened.

15 "The Truth Will Set You Free," whatenlightenment.net, posted April 22, 2009
16 "The Other Side of the Rainbow," andrewcohen.org/blog, posted May 12, 2009

This, then, is the rationale underlying Cohen's notion of "natural hierarchy," and that he uses to justify his position at its pinnacle: he is the One who never forgets. But I think it is fair to say that none of us have ever forgotten the impulse that prompted us to seek in the first place; what we sometimes *wish* we could forget are the outrageously unenlightened measures that Andrew Cohen continues to take in his struggle to maintain power and control over his followers.

Let me reiterate, though, that Andrew Cohen is not, at least in my estimation, an evil or demonic figure. He is, rather, someone who believes so fervently in his own fantasy of mastery that he attracts people who seek to strive with the same boundless confidence — which is why, in his community, the closer you get to the goal, the more clear it becomes that what you are climbing is that proverbial "mountain of shit under an inch of snow"; and why (EnlightenNext's latest "stabilization of higher consciousness" notwithstanding) Cohen's students are always rising and falling, never knowing for certain where they stand, and constantly having to reassure themselves that all the things they are seeing and hearing are manifestations of the Truth Absolute.

Yes, it *would* be funny if it were not also tragic, toxic and potentially dangerous. During the period in which my gag order was in effect, fear, concern, grief and frustration over this mess only grew in me, and while I have healed some of the rage, my sense of urgency remains. And I am by no means the only one; other former students are also aware of the full extent of the problem, which only a full accounting can help to heal, and without which a safe resolution may well prove impossible: A person so committed to his own delusions of grandeur, and so readily callous and abusive in their service, will never otherwise relinquish control.

2

THE BEGINNING

O N a snowy night in Amherst, Massachusetts, in March 1988, an old friend told me a remarkable story about an Eastern wise man and an American seeker. H.W.L. Poonja, a mystic sage in India, had transformed a young Westerner in a matter of weeks into a powerful guru who he had charged with inspiring "a revolution among the young."[17] After two years of teaching in England and Israel, the young guru had gathered a following of more than one hundred devoted students, and in 1988, had brought his spiritual revolution to Western Massachusetts. The guru's name was Andrew Cohen. Who was this enlightened American, I wondered? I was attracted to the notion that a regular guy, maybe even a guy like me, could achieve enlightenment. A longtime spiritual seeker, I also wondered whether Andrew Cohen was someone I might want to follow. Just a few days after hearing about him, I found my way to Andrew's living room for an evening *satsang*, or teaching.

At the time, my life was very full. I was newly married and living in a comfortable old farmhouse on a beautiful piece of land. I had a thriving real estate business and a twice-daily Buddhist meditation practice. I was a man with blessings to spare. Even so, I was aware of a spiritual poverty within me, an inability to claim what I most deeply needed and wanted from life. So when my friend told me about Andrew Cohen and his *satsangs*, I hurried to attend.

I will never forget that first *satsang*. Many people sat silently in anticipation of Andrew's arrival; a fellow next to me quietly boasted of having been a follower "from the beginning." When

---

17 Cohen, Andrew, *My Master Is Myself: The Birth of a Spiritual Teacher* (second edition), Lenox, MA: What Is Enlightenment? Press, 1995, p. 61

Andrew finally entered after twenty minutes or so, he advanced to the front of the room and sat, eyes closed, in a cushioned chair.

Eventually, he opened his eyes and said, "Does anyone have any questions?"

Many people did.

"What is the true nature of freedom?"

"What are the obstacles to achieving it?"

"How can I be free with all my responsibilities?"

I was struck by Andrew's serenity. He spoke broadly about spiritual freedom as the here and now, as one's very nature. He urged us to abandon the notion that we are not free. He promised that once we did, we would realize our true nature. His talk cast a spell on me. More than hear his words, I felt them. I felt that I, too, could be free, and I felt connected to my passionate desire to attain that freedom.

I returned nightly to Andrew Cohen's *satsangs,* which often lasted for many hours. Sometimes, Andrew sat in silence for the duration and left without saying a word. On other evenings, Andrew read letters that people had left by his chair. Most often, he solicited questions. I was profoundly moved by those evenings. I felt that I was bearing witness to a mystery that defied expression or comprehension.

My own exchanges with Andrew fed my deep yearning for freedom, which had been the object of my many years of spiritual practice. As I spent more time in Andrew's presence, the possibility of enlightenment seemed more tangible to me. One night, Andrew addressed me directly. He likened my quest for freedom to hanging from a rope over a deep pool of water — all I had to do was let go of the rope and fall in. How I wanted to fall! But the surrender required to do so eluded me.

"Bliss or no bliss," Andrew was fond of saying, "it's all bliss." From this perspective, I began to see through and beyond my limitations and conditioning. Andrew wove the non-duality teachings of Indian *Advaita Vedanta* into his discourses, and I was moved by the promise of perfection articulated in them. By the end of my first week of *satsang,* I was convinced that I myself could attain the highest spiritual goal: enlightenment. Andrew spoke compellingly of the immediacy of the directly experienced present, "right now" and "in this moment," and I believed that the awakened condition of the Buddha, the timeless serenity of saints and sages, was available for me to claim and experience as my own. I told myself, "Nothing is a problem; it is only that I believe in problems." Increasingly, a voice within me expressed a confidence that in Andrew and his teachings I had found my path.

One night after *satsang,* in a private meeting with Andrew, I expressed my desire to move closer to him and become more involved in his work. There was great power in the acknowledgment of our growing mutual trust, and he counseled me to stay the course. In time, he said, as the love between us grew, I would be drawn more deeply into his world. This was an affectionate and confidence-inspiring message that allowed my feelings of joy and optimism to expand. I was inspired, but I was also scared. I mourned the imminent death of my past even as I laughed aloud at the improbability of my life's sudden turn.

Inevitably, my gravitation toward Andrew strained my marriage. My wife attended several *satsangs* but was unmoved by what she witnessed there. Andrew addressed her fears that she would lose me, but offered no solace. "I've stolen Bill away from you!" he exclaimed to her on one occasion. My marriage broke down just four months after I'd attended my first *satsang,* and that is when I gave up everything. I moved into one of Andrew's group houses and embarked on what was to be a thirteen-year career as a devotee. From that moment forward, my life and Andrew's—his teachings, wishes and priorities—were profoundly intertwined.

My new community included students who had followed Andrew from England, Holland and Italy. Later that summer, our community of approximately 130 people moved to Boston. We held our nightly *satsangs* in the rented hall of a Montessori school across the Charles River in Cambridge. It was a new setting, but our dedication remained the same. The one thing missing was an influx of new students, so Andrew set his sights on finding more followers on the West Coast.

Heading West

After a successful speaking tour in California that had sparked interest in himself and his teachings, Andrew decided to resettle his community in the San Francisco Bay Area. By May of 1989, we were living in close quarters in a few rented houses in Marin County. Privacy had no currency for us; our focus was on our collective spiritual experience. Andrew inaugurated community-wide meditations at a local yoga studio, and as the closeness and trust between community members grew, I became convinced that I had truly found my spiritual home. Throughout my entire adult life, I had been a spiritual migrant of sorts, moving often to pursue new interests, relationships and possibilities. Membership in Andrew's group felt like balm for an aching soul.

While Northern California was our new home, Andrew himself traveled increasingly often, teaching and holding retreats as far away as India and Switzerland. He also traveled stateside to teach in Boulder, Seattle and New York City. It was while accompanying him on some of these trips that I befriended students from all over — London, Amsterdam, Israel and beyond — whom Andrew's message had begun to attract. With them came a vibrant and increasingly abundant energy that appeared to validate the collective commitment of those already involved. It was a time when anything seemed possible.

As Andrew's fame grew, so did our conviction that he was a "world teacher" after the fashion of J. Krishnamurti, who had been recognized as such during his youth in India, in 1910. Krishnamurti had spent his long life traveling all over the world advancing his philosophy and spiritual views, and Andrew envisioned himself in a similar role. To disseminate his teachings more widely, he founded a magazine, *What Is Enlightenment?* (recently rechristened *EnlightenNext*), created an editorial department for the publication of his books, vastly expanded his international teaching schedule, and increasingly relied on his students for creative, organizational and managerial support. Our work was neither optional nor remunerated; contributing to Andrew's success, our thinking went, was payment enough. Travel expenses incurred in the course of organizing and managing distant events were not reimbursed. It was regarded as a privilege to be tapped as traveling staff and to finance our own participation in Andrew's work.

For Andrew, however, this was still not enough. One night, as he and I were standing outside his house following a *satsang* in Marin, he said to me, "Bill, I could do much more. *So* much more." He often spoke of taking on a greater number of students, and of taking them "further." Despite the apparent success of his teaching trips, Andrew was frustrated with the size of the groups attending his teachings in California. He wanted more students, and as he set his sights on expansion beyond his existing community, he now sought also to impose more order within it.

I observed that as the scope of Andrew's ambition for recognition and a following grew beyond his immediate ability to fulfill it, he seemed to develop a need to control whatever he could, establishing order and structure where previously it had not been thought necessary. New rules signaled that changes — benign and otherwise — were beginning to take place within the community. Where, for example, Andrew had once regarded meditation as a nonessential ritual, he now decided to institute a mandatory daily meditation practice — along with, for some students, a daily practice of chanting passages from his writings. One such commonly assigned passage, "Pride is Vicious," when repeated 108 times, took nearly an hour to complete.

It was also in Marin that Andrew instituted weekly gender-segregated meetings. Conceived as forums in which community members could "investigate the teachings," these meetings gradually took on another purpose: targeted criticism — "feedback" in Andrew's parlance — of a fellow student, ostensibly to free that student from the influence of his or her ego. Such meetings could be grueling affairs lasting into the wee hours of the morning. If students did not humbly and sincerely embrace the offered criticism, they were labeled "resistant" and subjected to what Andrew referred to as "help" — amounting, essentially, to protracted attacks on their character by other students.

It became typical in Andrew's community for some student, deemed to have transgressed in some way, to be "taken on" by the group in the spirit of ruthless self-examination dictated by Andrew. At any given time someone was on the hot seat, and none of us ever knew when our turn might come. Early on, I was the focus of one such "feedback" session, having been accused of undermining a fellow student with whom I felt competitive. I became frightened and defensive — behaviors considered unacceptable in our forum — and I was subjected to several hours of intense and escalating pressure intended to humble me.

The day after my ordeal, which had concluded at 3 A.M., I received a directive from Andrew via his wife, Alka, to shave my head. Off came my hair, and off it stayed for four years. This was Andrew's remedy for pride or vanity, and he had already begun using it on other students. In some instances, he employed this tactic with students whose sexuality he deemed problematic, and after a while it came to be regarded as a symbol of sexual renunciation and celibacy; thus institutionalized, it was typically prescribed for a year at a time. Often, however, a perceived offense — a display of pride or aggressive behavior, for example — would result in a "renewal of vows": another year with a shaved head. My "vows" were extended in this fashion three times. While "stepping outside the sexual arena" for a period of time ostensibly created conditions conducive to enlightened understanding, enforced celibacy was also a powerful means of regimentation and control. Some members of the community spent up to seven years with their heads shaved.

Though vaguely aware of a creeping authoritarianism in Andrew's approach to spiritual leadership, I still felt happy and trustful of his motivations. I was involved in many aspects of community life, and over time I became one of Andrew's right-hand people, assisting him in a variety of ways. I traveled with him and was often given the responsibility of setting up teaching venues and scouting for possible facilities, eventually becoming a member of the Board of Directors. With the clarity of hindsight, I now see that the incremental changes taking place in Marin were harbingers of the more severe practices and strictures to come; but in the early 1990s, almost five years into my tenure as Andrew Cohen's student, I entertained no thoughts of leaving. As a way of life I still considered the balance of things to be tipped totally in the community's — and Andrew's — favor.

FINDING FOXHOLLOW

In 1994, Andrew put me in charge of a continent-wide search for a home, or *ashram,* for his growing community. He was disillusioned with the spiritual culture of Marin County and disappointed with the low volume of new recruits. My mission was to find a property that would facilitate both the attraction of new followers and the retention of current ones — a property that had plenty of room for growth. My early explorations in Northern California, Portland and Seattle didn't pan out. Andrew then redirected my focus to the East Coast, despite his past dissatisfaction with that region. In the summer of 1995, I moved with another student to High Falls, New York, in search of properties in the vicinity. The following winter we relocated to the Berkshire region of Western Massachusetts, and there, in Lenox, we found what we had been looking for: a 220-acre estate, formerly owned by the Vanderbilt family, that was to become the new world headquarters of Andrew's community, EnlightenNext.

Foxhollow, as the property is known, had been a subsidiary campus of the nearby Kripalu Yoga Center, which had been touched by scandal in 1993. Kripalu's founder and spiritual leader, Yogi Amrit Desai, who represented himself as a married celibate, preached celibacy and held his community to strict celibate vows, was revealed to have sexually exploited several of his female students. A major legal crisis ensued, forcing Kripalu to sell Foxhollow in order to settle a series of claims by long-term members that had brought the organization to the brink of bankruptcy.

At close to $3,000,000, the purchase of Foxhollow required far more funds than Andrew's organization had available. Andrew was counting on the largesse of a wealthy student, Jane O'Neil, who had earlier offered a loan toward the purchase of a new property. Instead, Andrew now asked Jane to consider donating the money. She was due to receive $2,000,000 from the distribution of a family trust. Andrew charged Mikaela, a senior student who was also one of Jane's closest friends in the community, with bringing her around to the idea of donating rather than lending the entire amount. While deeply devoted to Andrew, Jane was hesitant about parting with such a vast sum of money. She was worried in particular about the prospect of her relatives' disapproval were they to discover the use to which she had put her share of the family fortune.

During a weekend community retreat in Northern California, Mikaela met with Jane several times and gradually persuaded her to finance the purchase. Already self-conscious about her wealth and concerned about the possibility of undue appreciation or preferential treatment resulting from her generosity, Jane stipulated that the donation be kept strictly confidential, a measure that would also insulate her against the possibility of her family finding out. Andrew agreed. Jane then convinced the relative in charge of the trust to release the funds earlier than scheduled, despite considerable financial penalties and loss of interest income.

A few months later, the wired funds arrived at the local bank, and the 220-acre property was officially "ours." I have a photo of a beaming Jane O'Neil standing together with myself and an architect who was a longtime student of Andrew's in front of the Foxhollow Manor House. That photo is an awkward relic for me now; I cannot look at it without cringing at the memory of how Jane was manipulated while I stood by without objecting in any way. Within two years, Jane had left the community.

Soon after the purchase of Foxhollow, a small advance team from California joined us to begin preliminary renovations. We shared a winter of good company and hard work as we prepared the site for the arrival of the full community from Marin the following spring. Our plan was to restore Foxhollow while adapting it to our own purposes. The main building, the Manor House, occupied more than 30,000 square feet. Additional structures included four houses, a twelve-room guesthouse and thirty-six apartments in three separate buildings.

The architect had designed a complex $1,000,000 conversion of the property, and by the spring of 1997, many students were arriving in Lenox to help with the project. Things progressed quickly, and I was thrilled. It was one of the happiest times of my career, and of my relationship with Andrew. I became Foxhollow's business manager, a member of its Board of Directors, and sat on the committee that directed major upgrades to its infrastructure. I was the Board's liaison with the investment advisor who managed the organization's growing portfolio. I also lived in Andrew's house, the only student other than his wife who shared that privilege.

For many years, the promise of enlightenment had sustained us, along with the deep love and trust that flourished among community members. Now, as Andrew's profile began to rise, and as our student community grew, the number of practices, meetings and projects around which our days and nights were organized began to multiply. Seldom in my life had I been so busy, so focused, but I felt purpose-driven in what struck me as a wholesome and unprecedented way, like an athlete "in the zone," poised to break a record. During this time, Andrew often spoke about "an absolute relationship to life" as a feature of the enlightened condition, and as his students, we were committed to the cultivation of an "all hands on deck" attitude. Working at this level of commitment and efficiency was often thrilling.

Nearly a decade had passed since my first encounter with Andrew Cohen on that snowy March night in 1988. I cherished my leadership role in his community, and I marveled at my life's trajectory. In many ways—and for the first time in my life—I felt fulfilled. Foxhollow was my home, my fellow students were my family, and Andrew was my spiritual mentor. Yet not everything was as it seemed. In addition to new rules and practices that seemed to contradict some of Andrew's earlier teachings, money began to have a growing influence on day-to-day life at Foxhollow. Just prior to the opening of the new *ashram,* Andrew had instituted an entrance fee of $1000 per formal student for *each year* of prior participation as such. The collection of this fee had helped to finance renovations at Foxhollow, while entitling the student/donors to live there and to participate in community events. (For some, it was a burden; one is still paying off the $8000 she put on her credit card in 1997.)

Thus, with the gradual imposition of rules, taxes and spirit-breaking confrontational meetings, the climate in Andrew's community had changed significantly, and the man who had once seemed to me to embody perfection was slowly revealing another side of his character. As the community took root at Foxhollow, I began to witness transformations in Andrew's personality, methods and teachings that would take me years to fully comprehend. But in 1997, with a gleaming new facility, a growing community, and my own personal sense of accomplishment, Foxhollow was still where I wanted to be. At that point, I could not see the storm clouds gathering on the horizon.

3

THE DARK SIDE OF ENLIGHTENMENT

The modern spiritual world has been plagued by countless shocking revelations of that vital discrepancy between word and deed. This has created an air of cynicism and a crisis of trust. It should cause the independent thinker to question the ultimate validity of the attainment of those in whom these discrepancies have become painfully obvious. Yet I have been intrigued by the general lack of serious inquiry into this important question.

–Andrew Cohen[18]

S OME of the changes in our new environment were subtle, such as the institution of a daily exercise regime, and some, while they were closely guarded secrets occurring only behind closed doors, were not subtle at all, such as punishment in the form of physical abuse. From the most benign to the most damaging, these changes were indicative of the power that Andrew Cohen sought to exert on his followers' lives. They were also harbingers of even more egregious abuses to come.

What accounted for these developments? In part, locale. Whereas in Marin we had existed as part of a larger community and interacted with the world around us, at Foxhollow our community was completely self-contained. Inside the *ashram*, while the lives of students were much easier to insulate from "non-spiritual" distractions and influences, they were also much easier to control. By mandating daily physical activity, Andrew imposed a directive on his followers while subtracting a quota of their personal choice. Thus the benefits of a daily exercise program—in my case, working up the strength and stamina to complete a marathon on my fiftieth birthday—came at the price of personal free-

---

18 Cohen, Andrew, *An Unconditional Relationship to Life: The Odyssey of an American Spiritual Teacher*, Lenox, MA: What Is Enlightenment? Press, 1995, p. 47 (online: "A Crisis of Trust," enlightennext.org/magazine/j9/andrew_crisis.asp)

dom, and while I was troubled by this, it seemed undeniable to me that the benefits outweighed the cost.

Andrew was in a position to expand the degree of control he exercised in increments that went undetected — perhaps even by him, if one cares to give him the benefit of the doubt. Now, in addition to micromanaging the fitness regimes of each of his students, it was apparent that their sexual and romantic lives represented an arena equally subject to his influence. While I had tolerated the former because I had clearly benefited from it, when Andrew began taking control of my romantic partnerships — including who to have a relationship with and when to end it — my acquiescence was more grudging.

Romantic love was already elusive in the community. Various rules had long dictated everything from eligibility to acceptable conduct. Only members of approximately equal rank, for example, could partner with each other. As a long-term member with leadership responsibilities, I could only seek companionship among the few women who had proven themselves through years of devotion and service to Andrew. No one was allowed to seek a partner outside the community, there was no form of ritualized dating within it, and there were no casual sexual encounters. As a result, I spent all but six months of my thirteen years with Andrew without a romantic partner. When one did manage to obtain permission for a relationship, as I did for just a few months, Andrew often intervened. In my case, he decided that my relationship should end because my partner had been "proud," thus earning his disapproval. In other words, like all relationships inside the community, mine began with his consent and ended by his decree.

Along with new rules and regulations and expanded control over our private lives, Andrew also began instituting punishments as well. The methods were often random, harsh, out of proportion to the alleged wrong, and questionable as educational or disciplinary "skillful means." Andrew referred to his updated version of "crazy wisdom" — a teaching modality with centuries-old roots in some Eastern spiritual traditions — as "Acts of Outrageous Integrity," and it consisted of extreme "teaching methods" designed to cut through a student's ego and resistance in order to facilitate awakening.

In an interview in an early issue of Andrew Cohen's own magazine, *What Is Enlightenment?*, the spiritual teacher Lee Lozowick remarked:

> ...[T]he teachers who I call charlatans today are teachers who are completely irresponsible in their use of power and crazy manifestation. I would consider a crazy-wisdom teacher someone who might use anything, but who is never arbitrary, and never follows their own personal motives. They only use dramatic and shocking manifestations under specific circumstances at exactly the right time... A crazy-wisdom teacher is a master at faceting. A charlatan is someone who just takes the hammer and chisel and wails away and hopes that there are some beneficial results—or maybe doesn't even care but just loves the euphoria of the exercise of power and people groveling at his or her feet.[19]

In apparent agreement, Andrew Cohen himself has remarked that crazy wisdom seems to be an excuse for some teachers to engage irresponsibly in self-indulgent behavior (of course exempting himself from this characterization), and in meetings with students he outlined the following very sensible criteria for its application: The sole goal of the implementation of unconventional or seemingly inappropriate methods is the liberation of the student; there can be no suggestion of the teacher's personal benefit or pleasure; the sole criterion for success is the student's liberation — only then can crazy wisdom be considered authentic and effective.

Yet Cohen's by now customary defense against allegations directed at himself personally — of abuse masquerading as crazy wisdom — consists of splitting hairs over definitions of terms,[20] recourse to the larger controversy regarding the validity of crazy wisdom itself that has existed for some time in East-meets-West spiritual debate, and a disarmingly unreflective attempt to cast

---

19 *What Is Enlightenment?* magazine, v. 20, Fall/Winter 2001
20 See *Chapter 14*, Yonatan Levy's "interview" with EnlightenNext.

himself as someone who is unafraid to appear politically incorrect in his heroic effort to do what his job description demands of him.[21] It is abundantly clear from the ostensible views of both Lozowick and Cohen, however, that crazy wisdom as a tradition has a set of implicit guidelines by means of which to judge the actions of any teacher purporting to use it; there is thus no escape from the impressions and evaluations of others, no "free pass" just because someone is supposedly "enlightened," or claims to have the best interests of others at heart and is willing to use extreme methods in order to "free them from ignorance."

Regarding many examples of the extreme measures sometimes taken by Andrew Cohen at Foxhollow, students have since stated that far from being freed from their own ignorance, they had been subjected to a new and pernicious version of someone else's. Cohen's "acts of outrageous integrity" included disciplinary face slapping — usually in response to a student's performance of some task failing to measure up to his expectations — in which it was difficult to discern any particular "lesson" other than "Shape up!" This practice began soon after our arrival at Foxhollow. In some cases, Andrew would direct one student to slap another; in others, he administered the slaps himself. I myself was slapped on two occasions, once by a woman and once by another man.

For some time, Cohen had also been bestowing ironic spiritual names intended to make their bearers acutely aware of their character flaws. There were Mad Dog and Raging Bull, who had tempers; Pleiades, who was "detached"; Nar, who was "narcissistic"; Cas, who was "casual"; His Greatness (H.G. for short), who was "arrogant"; Integrity, who supposedly lacked it; and Sincere, who supposedly wasn't. Other names included Dizzy and Mephisto. While these may or may not have been helpful, naming itself is understood by sociologists and psychologists to constitute a powerful means of indoctrination and social control, and it certainly had such an effect on our collective consciousness.

---

21 "A Declaration of Integrity," andrewcohen.org/blog, posted October 18, 2006

These practices—which some might well regard as instances of physical and mental abuse—were symptoms of the unprecedented degree of control that eventually came to pervade the atmosphere of the Foxhollow community, and "groupthink" was certainly a consequence of this atmosphere of control. It is a well-known and troubling fact that group mentality has the potential to override individual morality. I experienced this firsthand as a member of Andrew Cohen's community—observing, participating in, rationalizing and excusing, at times, extremely harsh treatment of fellow members who had angered their teacher. When a student was slapped or evicted from a student household, for example, I told myself that it was for that individual's own good, chalking it up to my teacher's passionate determination to free him or her from a confining limitation, or from the tyranny of the ego. I also sometimes rationalized such treatment as an appropriate consequence of failing to live up to Andrew's standards and teachings. I do not regard the fact that there was no forum in which to question such behavior as an excuse for my failure to have done so. Even when, later on, I found myself on the receiving end of abusive treatment, I "compartmentalized" these experiences in my own mind, suspending judgment—and my own humanity—in an effort to adhere to the party line.

Face slapping and name-calling, while they were uncalled for and may have been damaging, were mild in comparison to other questionable manifestations of "crazy wisdom" that occurred at Foxhollow. One such incident involved a student (Mikaela) who was responsible for the marketing of Andrew's publications and who had fallen out of favor by reminding him that something he had criticized her for doing had been his idea in the first place. He decried her as evil and ordered that the walls, floor and ceiling of her office (which had been relocated to an unfinished basement room) be painted red to signify the spilled blood of her guru. She was ordered to spend hours there contemplating the implications of her transgression, with the additional aid of a large cartoon on the wall depicting her as a vampire and the word "traitor" written in large letters next to it.

Andrew often employed red paint in this fashion to create environments designed to induce shame and guilt in students that he felt had questioned his judgment or disobeyed him. Another female student who had displeased Andrew and, after leaving the community, had returned to help out on a weekend painting project, was summoned to another basement room. There she was met by four female students who, having guided her onto a plastic sheet on the floor, each poured a bucket of paint over her head as a "message of gratitude" from Andrew. She left the property traumatized and fell ill in subsequent days (during which she was harassed by phone calls from another student who, at Cohen's instigation, repeatedly called her a "coward") and never again returned to Foxhollow.

"Crazy wisdom" is the most charitable possible explanation for these often traumatic and disturbing incidents, many of which have already been related on the whatenlightenment.net blog. Several of these student accounts of Andrew Cohen's "acts of outrageous integrity," employed to dubious or damaging effect, are reproduced below.

I was living at the Foxhollow center in 2001 when Stan Brady, at that time a leader at the London Center, was suddenly ordered to come to Foxhollow. Andrew told some of us that Stan had been "doing things his own way" for a while, and now had directly disobeyed him. Andrew was furious, and we all knew from past experience that Steve would be in for it when he got to Foxhollow. When he arrived, he was an emotional mess, expressing apologies to Andrew and feeling very guilty. The "horrible thing" that he had done was to give some advice to one of the formal students in London despite Andrew's instructions not to.

First, Andrew had me and another student speak with Stan in an intensely confrontational way. As usual, we were then to report to Andrew on whether he was "coming through," i.e., responding appropriately. Of course Stan, who was frightened and cut off from his own emotions, was as unresponsive as any normal human being would be under such circumstances; for Andrew and ourselves, however, habituated as we were to confrontational strategies for "meeting with someone," Stan's failure to own up to his "competition" with Andrew meant that he was not "taking responsibility." Then Andrew himself met with Stan, treating him coldly and condescendingly (even though Stan was literally bowing to him when he entered his room) because his profuse apologies struck Andrew as "unreal."

Next, we were instructed to call Stan back to Andrew's residence, where his wife Alka had been told not to "hold back" and to "really go for it with Stan." I was just outside the house, and I could hear her screaming at Stan and punching him. It was a chilling experience to listen to him crying and moaning his apologies as Alka beat him while screaming loudly, "How dare you betray Andrew? How dare you?" Afterward, Andrew told me proudly, "Alka really went for it with Stan!"

Subjected to such harsh discipline, people who were strong leaders in Andrew's community often became beaten down, weakened and humiliated. (This was the condition I ultimately left in as well.) As for Stan, shortly after the beating by Alka, Cohen demoted him and then kicked him out of the community. Stan stayed around for more than a year, living a strange existence on the fringes of Foxhollow and working as an orderly at a local hospital, occasionally sending flowers and apologies to Andrew—who during this period had me and others call Stan on the phone to "mess with his mind." Listening to Stan on his speakerphone, Andrew would coach us on what to say or laugh silently, giving thumbs-up signs as all this was going on. I am sickened that I went along with these tormenting tactics, but we all did such things to each other under Andrew's direction. During this time, Andrew would say how much he hated Stan, calling him "the devil," "Judas" and other such names. One night, he had me and [a] fellow student…go to Stan's residence and let the air out of all of his tires so that he couldn't get to work. He represented himself as trying to break down Stan's ego, but in retrospect it is obvious to me that Andrew was simply acting out his own vengeful anger at a perceived "betrayal."

This went on and on. At one point, Stan wrote to Andrew, saying that he would do anything to be allowed to come back…. In response to Stan's desperate letter, Andrew had him come to a remote part of Fox-hollow with instructions to start digging a deep 6 x 8-foot trench in the woods using only a shovel. At that time Andrew was into making videos of students who weren't "doing well" in an effort to capture what he called "the smile of the ego." (This is a whole story in itself; Andrew was convinced that when someone is under pressure to speak about what they're doing wrong, a "smile" emerges like that of "the devil himself.") Andrew had me drive a golf cart carrying him, his dog and one of the EnlightenNext videographers…to the site of the huge trench where we found Stan, standing about five feet below us, hunched over his shovel and drenched in sweat. He seemed startled to actually see his teacher after such a long period of excommunication. As he paused from his digging, Stan looked up at Andrew with an expression of reverence and said hello—but he looked like a broken man, not at all the person I knew.

It was a sad picture, the more horrifying because Andrew just stood there looking down at him, holding his little dog in his arms and telling us coldly, "There's the devil smiling at me," and instructing [the videographer] to get the camera rolling. I remember him saying, "Look how cut off he is, happy to be down there digging. There's no love in his eyes." Yet it was Andrew who seemed bereft of any love, compassion or humanity. In my mind—though now I see it differently—I still actually believed he was trying to help Stan.[22]

Some years ago at Foxhollow, a student named Jeff, a very good writer, was having a great deal of trouble with a writing project he had been assigned to do. He was supposed to write an introduction to a book Andrew was publishing, but he was having no success. Feeling terrible guilt about this, he wrote in a desperate letter to Andrew, "If I don't come through, I will cut my finger off." Andrew seemed to like this idea. When Jeff still did not succeed at his writing, Andrew called for Mikaela, [who was a] physician, to come see him…. Andrew told Mikaela to go

22 whatenlightenment.net, posted April 22, 2009

to see Jeff, and to bring her medical kit. She was instructed to tell Jeff that Andrew was taking him up on his offer to sacrifice a finger. She should take out her scalpel, her mask, her gloves, a sponge—everything she would need for such an operation—and lay them all out. She was told to carry through the charade up to the very last minute, and then stop.

When Mikaela visited Jeff, he had barely slept in about a week. He was in a desperate state.... Mikaela [later] confirmed...that she had followed Andrew's instructions precisely. Jeff was severely and obviously shaken by the incident. He left Andrew and Foxhollow a few weeks later.[23]

For a period of time, Andrew occasionally sent close students, individually, to the lake to chant some affirmation or repentance while repeatedly submerging themselves in the water. I had done this two times before.... One time it took one hour, and the other time it took over three hours to complete the assigned number of chants/submersions. Both of these incidents were in the warm summer months. So, while very challenging (especially the time it took—three-plus hours!), it was not dangerous. (Reflecting on it now, though, I find both of those teaching directives from Andrew very unhelpful responses to what was happening with me at those times.)

The lake incident...was different in that it involved many women at once, and it was in October. The lake was not yet frozen but it was very, very cold. Fall and winter come quickly in the Berkshires.... The women were "in trouble" for an indiscretion, and we were falling all over ourselves to come up with a gesture of apology and repentance to Andrew. One of the women suggested that we go *en masse* to do prostrations in the lake. A message was sent to Andrew that this was our intention. He accepted and then sent a couple of directives about it. So while he did not exactly order us to do it, once we had offered to do it he became quite involved. Women who did not complete the exercise were ordered to go back and do it again—supervised, to make sure that

23 whatenlightenment.net, posted March 24, 2005

they remained in the lake the whole hour. At least one woman had to go back a third time. Because I was one of the few women who had already done this twice, I just gritted my teeth and tried to muscle through it. However, I was immediately shocked by how cold the water was.

At that time in the community, when you received word that Andrew wanted you to go do "prostrations" in the lake, you went immediately in whatever you were wearing. I was wearing cotton pants and a cotton shirt, neither of which provided any warmth. I also had a shaved head. I believe that the women with shaved heads had a bit more difficulty with the cold. I just forced myself to continue even as I found it harder and harder to keep my balance and was becoming increasingly "blank." I then have a very vague memory of being pushed into a car. The next thing I remember was regaining consciousness propped up in a shower stall with three other women, all of us standing under the hot water trying to regain enough feeling in our hands to unbutton our clothes and pull them off of us. I had lost consciousness at about 50 or 55 minutes, just shy of the full hour. I am told that one woman who was watching and didn't go in because she was recovering from a bad chest cold (Alka, Andrew's wife), and a couple of women who had said "Enough!" and had come out early (and therefore had to go back and repeat the exercise a couple of days later), noticed that I was losing consciousness and had me pulled out of the water.

It took two days for me to feel normal again. I do feel that this was one of the more dangerous things that Andrew had his students do. Many of the women who participated say it was one of the most extreme things they have ever experienced in the community. I think it may have been worse for me because I had been in a serious car accident less than a year earlier and had suffered a severe concussion. I was continuing to have regular follow-up doctor's appointments and EEGs for a year following the accident, which included the period of the October lake incident. I find this one of Andrew's most ham-handed responses as a teacher, subjecting a large group of women to the same giant hammer without regard for what would be appropriate and useful for *individuals*. I also acknowledge how stupid and sheeplike it was for me to participate.[24]

A FINAL WORD ON CRAZY WISDOM

"…I don't hesitate to say," Andrew has declared, "that for the sake of individual or collective development, I definitely have at times pushed my students very hard—not for personal gain and, indeed, always at tremendous personal risk."[25] But because (characteristically) the "personal risk" Andrew is willing to acknowledge is to himself or his projects rather than to the students he is "pushing," the work of healing the long-term damage inflicted by his directives lands by default on the people whose minds and bodies absorb them, and on the consciences of the trusting onlookers who collude through their silence. Many of us who have left the community have discussed among ourselves our complicity in the meting out of punishments and the execution of "crazy wisdom acts" that essentially amounted to abuse, and whether we witnessed these abuses firsthand or from a distance, we have often expressed regret over our failure to intervene or to acknowledge our part in the harm they brought to so many individuals.

In early 1998, for example, Andrew told me about a conversation he'd recently had with two of his close male students. They had been in a sauna together when Andrew began lamenting the fact that his female students collectively (including, presumably, his own wife) were "not doing well," and "might not make it." Andrew—by his own account—had then suggested that the three of them drop their women and spend the following evening with some prostitutes; but they hadn't followed through because he had woken up the next morning with a bad case of the flu.

I was completely shocked and had no idea what to make of this. Then, a few days later, Andrew ordered one of these male

24 whatenlightenment.net, posted April 22, 2009
25 "A Declaration of Integrity," andrewcohen.org/blog, posted October 18, 2006

students, John, to terminate his relationship with his partner. However "normal" such situations had become for us as Andrew's students, John was now in the difficult position of having to accept his teacher's unilateral verdict on a relationship that he cherished, and after several weeks it emerged that in his traumatized emotional state he had thought back to Andrew's idea in the sauna and decided to console himself with prostitutes on his own.

When Andrew heard about this several weeks later, he expressed outrage and decided to teach John a lesson: he ordered him to visit prostitutes frequently as a formal "spiritual practice." Andrew was quite proud of this crazy-wise prescription, and though John begged repeatedly to be relieved of his obligations, Andrew took this as a negative indication with respect to John's "attitude," and showed no willingness to relent.

I recognize now that when I had first heard Andrew's unsolicited recollection of the discussion in the sauna — which was at least several days before he ended John's relationship, and weeks before he had even begun considering this bizarre "teaching strategy" — it would have been a perfectly sensible act on my part to ask Andrew if he had been serious about visiting prostitutes in the first place. Yet I refrained from questioning my teacher not only at that time but during the entire period when this "idea" of his was wreaking such havoc in John's life and evolving into a full-blown "spiritual practice" to be imposed on a powerless and suggestible disciple who was grief-stricken over the loss of his girlfriend. And as if all this were not enough, once John's ordeal had begun in earnest, I participated with several other men in a long distance conference call during which, at Andrew's urging, we chided John for failing to approach this "opportunity to face into his sexuality" with "the right spirit."

It had of course occurred to me, given the apparent circumstances, that John's mistake might not have been visiting prostitutes in itself so much as having done so under his own auspices; yet whatever inner qualms any of us might have had, no one — myself included — ever raised any objection to the profound compromises that John was now being forced to make. And Andrew's own recent denial of these events — among so many others that he also denies[26] — has possibly helped me to make sense of the final comment I ever heard from him on the whole episode: that if John had been able to keep his secret to himself, Andrew wouldn't have been forced to respond as he had.

Thus, as Andrew Cohen's "acts of outrageous integrity" became a common fixture in our community, some students looked on as others were subjected to increasingly outlandish forms of discipline, and the resulting toll on the mental and emotional condition of all concerned was great.[27] Yet despite the severity of these "spiritual practices," redemption rarely followed, and it was gradually becoming apparent that the guru's renewed good graces came at an entirely different sort of price. The chapter that follows explores the advent of this new "currency of forgiveness" at EnlightenNext: cold, hard cash.

---

26 See *Chapter 14*, Yonatan Levy's "interview" with EnlightenNext.
27 On some level, apparently, it was also difficult for Andrew himself, who sometimes greeted students he had summoned to a local bar for criticism with the remark, "I called you here because I have to get drunk before I can talk to you!" (whatenlightenment.net, reported January 11, 2006)

4

THE CURRENCY OF FORGIVENESS

T HE move to Foxhollow represented a new and unfamiliar
undertaking for Andrew Cohen and his students. Moving
from small rented offices and houses in Marin County to
a new 220-acre facility with accommodations for up to a hundred,
plus a main building of over 30,000 square feet, was a jump that
was thrilling for us as participants, and also quite a lot to digest
and take responsibility for. The new venue would require a far
greater infusion of capital than we were accustomed to, and in
response Andrew set about creating new sources of funding.
EnlightenNext insists to this day that all of its funding has been
generated through voluntary donations only;[28] yet the accounts
presented below tell a vastly different story.

EnlightenNext also denies — contrary to the facts — that it was
ever customary for Andrew Cohen's students to buy him valuable gifts,[29] which in fact was common practice from the early
days of the community, and may well continue as such to this
day. During my tenure there, it was quite common for students
to buy Andrew expensive gifts on almost any occasion, and especially common as a gesture of apology after having in some
manner earned his disapproval. The student body as a whole pur-
chased a new Volvo for Andrew in 1996, although he already had
the use of a perfectly serviceable Honda Accord, and in 1998, on
the occasion of my tenth anniversary as his student, I gave him a
gift of $10,000 cash — which seemed to me at the time a perfectly
appropriate gesture of gratitude to my spiritual teacher.

The practice of donating money to atone for mistakes had begun in Marin in the mid-1990s, and at that time had been accepted
by all and never questioned or challenged. The first time I became
aware of its having evolved into official policy was after the move

---

28, 29 See *Chapter 14*, Yonatan Levy's "interview" with EnlightenNext.

to Foxhollow. Following Jane O'Neil's $2,000,000 "donation" and the Foxhollow "entrance fee" assessed from every individual formal student based on duration of prior community involvement, money held unprecedented sway within Andrew's community after its relocation east. Beyond the usual expenses of running a nonprofit organization, there were now new costs to be absorbed by students — arbitrary punitive penalties that defied categorization on any balance sheet.

In response to an inquiry by journalist Yonatan Levy about whether large donations from students were ever solicited under pressure, the official response of EnlightenNext's "Communications Director," Amy Edelstein, was as follows: "No, students are absolutely not put under pressure to give large sums of money. That would go against everything that EnlightenNext and Andrew Cohen stand for. All donations are given freely, and the vast majority of our donations are small."[30] My own observation, as one privy to every detail of the Foxhollow purchase and its subsequent administration and management, was that while Andrew was very moved by the new opportunity that the property represented — because he believed it was going to "put him on the map" — he also felt that his students in particular were now obligated to support his ambitions financially. He may even feel inwardly sincere in his representation that no pressure was brought to bear to the extent that, from his point of view, it was his students' *obligation*, rather than any grosser form of third-party manipulation, that compelled their "generosity."

But however Andrew Cohen may justify it to himself and his Board of Directors, what I witnessed, and what others have also reported, are clear indications of his recognition that he was going to have to venture beyond a purely voluntary basis for the collection of donations if his organization was to thrive. And if there had ever been any doubt prior to the community's relocation to Foxhollow, there was none thereafter: Money, not spirit, was the new coin of the realm. Beyond any concerns as mundane

30 See *Chapter 14*, Yonatan Levy's "interview" with EnlightenNext.

as operating overhead, money now became a key component of the spiritual path for Andrew's students. Just as the Catholic Church had once sold "indulgences" to sinners seeking absolution, so Andrew now began attaching price tags to his forgiveness for perceived wrongs.

Andrew let it be understood that his good favor could also be had for a price, establishing a practice that was morally reprehensible, legally questionable and indicative of a degree of corruption that had warped his ideals and would eventually stain the fabric of his entire organization. It is a testament to the faith that so many of us had in Andrew that, despite the questionable nature of these new financial arrangements, we complied — some of us taking on enormous and ill-advised debt. Though it may be difficult for outsiders to comprehend, our desire to please our guru was so great that we were prepared to mortgage our futures in order to do so.

Here again, the accounts on the whatenlightenment.net blog reproduced below — the first of which is excerpted from a letter addressed directly to Andrew Cohen — paint a composite picture of financial exploitation that is both revealing and deeply disturbing.

The following downward spiral would occur on more than one occasion: (1) your unreasonable demand on my time and dwindling resources, followed by (2) my unexpressed resentment, and ultimate "failure to produce," leading to (3) your overly intense expression of outrage toward me for the personal betrayal of you, for which I was put under enormous pressure by you and my fellow students to feel remorse, while making some gesture of contrition to you. As you well know, this psychological pressure and manipulation from you and others would even extend to being physically slapped in the face repeatedly, and verbally insulted and humiliated (often by women) until I could be "trusted" to turn over a new leaf. But at no time was I able to question you or your methods because I knew that at any time, if I didn't comply, I could be out on my ear, ostracized and even shunned by all my friends of fifteen years.... I have seen this sort of banishment happen to many others, and knew the anger and even hatred you harbored for those older students who left the community and/or, according to you, didn't give you all their time, attention, respect, obedience and at times even their money.

Under the psychological intensity and despair of one of these early cycles with you, I was struggling to prove to you that I cared enough, and so took the course that had by then become the prescribed means of getting out of hot water with you, showing remorse and proving how much one cared—offering you money.

In desperation I wrote you a check for $3,000.... I remember distinctly when you received my offer, you stormed into my room, angrily throwing the check to the floor and shouting at me dramatically, "Do you think you can buy me off for a lousy three grand?" I was flabbergasted. Could it be that there was an amount that I was expected to give that would show the necessary amount of intention and resolve to change? The right amount of care for you? I remembered a time when buying you flowers was a symbol for this; but times had changed, and now the currency of forgiveness and intention apparently was cash.

As you well know, I was around to watch as many others who "bottomed out," and wanting to prove their sincerity, felt pressured by you to buy their way back into your good graces. In fact, any longtime student in the community knew that sooner or later a "donation" would be required as the only way to resolve matters if they ever got into real trouble with you. Extracting "donations" from your students generally took place at a time when they felt victimized, emotionally overwrought, guilty, and trying to gain back your love, trust and affection. You actually even said to me and a few others at one time that when a 'committed' or a 'senior' student "blows it," it'll cost them $20,000 in *karmic* retribution. And all this, of course, normally happened without the slightest regard on your part for the student's actual financial situation. As appallingly manipulative and abusive as I now see your attitude to be, I knew that this was still the accepted way that things operated around you up until the time I left.

So, despite grave reservations about being able to do what your "rules" dictated in this situation, I dug deep, cleared out my bank account, borrowing the rest, and offered you what I thought would surely show my heart was in the right place—a check for $20,000. It was accepted and deposited by you. (This was followed by another pledge of $10,000 made to you a bit later when I was in London after having failed once again to meet all that you were demanding of me. I paid you $500 toward this at that time.)

I now find it all quite twisted and sickening. The benefit of leaving has afforded me the clarity I never had while in your world, and under the constant duress of enforced compliance to your wishes (being told this was for my liberation). So, now I am making a different and sane choice on my own behalf: Without further elaboration of past events, I simply and directly ask you to return my money to me now in full—$20,500— without conditions. This money can by no stretch of the imagination be considered a good faith donation to a nonprofit group, having been extracted from me under some of the most intense and extreme psychological stress imaginable.[31]

A friend of mine, a close student of Andrew's and a fellow leader in his community…[who] is presently one of the main officers in the EnlightenNext organization…"broke his vow" of celibacy, meaning in this case that he masturbated. Subsequently, he broke down and confessed this to Andrew, who was very upset and angry with him. My friend felt so guilty over this that he offered to give Andrew his inheritance to show how sorry he was. This offer was accepted, but the inheritance was not yet available. The last thing my friend told me at the time was that he was meeting with his family to request to borrow a sum of money as an advance on his inheritance. Can such a "donation" possibly be construed as "given freely"? Or was it encouraged and exploited as a sad and fearful gesture of forgiveness? To me, the answer is obvious.[32]

I cashed out a $60,000 IRA (Individual Retirement Account) and gave it to Andrew under severe pressure. These are the circumstances: In

---

31 whatenlightenment.net, posted February 7, 2005
32 whatenlightenment.net, posted April 22, 2009

July of 2000 I left the community—snuck out and ran away. I rented a car and just started driving, in a pretty distraught state. I ended up in New Orleans. Andrew tracked me down (that's a long story in itself) and I was persuaded to return to Massachusetts. Still in a pretty volatile state, I was assigned to stay with two other women who were also "in trouble" off-campus (or "off the property"). We rented a room in a boarding house. Over the next weeks, with daily messages and input from Andrew and his representatives, I came to be persuaded that I had made a horrible mistake in trying to leave, and I came to believe that Andrew was showing unfathomable generosity in trying to "save me from myself." I came to genuinely want to return to community life. We were living as pariahs in a kind of no-man's-land. I was told that in order to return, I had to give everything. I responded in various ways, offering what I thought was everything—spiritually, mentally, emotionally, physically. I offered some money, a few thousand dollars, thinking I would take it off my credit card. But I was told that it was not enough: "Everything means *everything*." I had an IRA that my father had been putting money into over many years. It was in my name, but my father was in control of it. It was to be a retirement account—exactly what the name says—because my father knew I wasn't making or saving any money and wasn't likely to, given the life I had chosen. Andrew was aware that I had an IRA; he knew everything about us. I eventually realized that this was what Andrew was asking for. After some inner struggle, I finally offered it. It was accepted, but then there was another message: "Everything is *everything*." It was then that I also offered any future inheritance I would receive from my family.

I was allowed to return to the community. I told Andrew's representative that it would take some time to make the arrangements. I had to persuade my father to turn the management of the account over to me. (I lied to him and told him that I wanted to put the money in more socially responsible investments.) Andrew followed up through his rep...numerous times to pressure me to speed up the process. Andrew's rep did say when I finally turned over the money that if I left the community again within the next year, I could get it back. At that time, I definitely did not think that I would ever leave the community again, and so I refused the offer, which I believe had been suggested by Andrew's rep in light of Bill Yenner's request (recent at that time) for the return of his inheritance.

Here is how I feel about it now, and why I did not try to get the money back when I did finally leave the community. It's tricky. First, I feel that Andrew's very strong pressure on me for the large donation when I was in an *extremely* vulnerable position was totally wrong. Such gifts must be given freely and not coerced, but coercion is exactly what Andrew did. Second, at the same time, I was a spiritual student who was celibate and had in a real sense "renounced the world." I was much like a nun in any tradition, and many spiritual paths require vows of poverty; so, in the scheme of the history of spiritual practice, being expected to give up everything is not so unusual. Third, the actual experience of giving up everything was very profound for me. I really did abandon the future and surrender much more deeply to my commitment to the spiritual path. Fourth, when I considered asking for the money back within the first year of my leaving the community, I was still too traumatized by the experience of finally leaving to have the strength and clarity to ask for the money to be returned. And, although I felt that Andrew's pressuring me to give the money was wrong, I felt that what I personally came to when I finally "gave everything" was something that I wanted to honor and stand behind. I rejected Andrew's coercive actions in the matter, but wanted to honor and take responsibility for my own intentions and actions.[33]

GAGGED

As I recount in greater detail elsewhere in this book, I also had the experience of buying forgiveness. In 1999, after eleven years of discipleship, I was judged to be "doing poorly," presumably because of my pride. I had been a leader in Andrew's community when, suddenly, I was exiled from Foxhollow. My isolation, which alternated for some time with "contact" in the form of vicious verbal attacks from other students, took such a severe toll

---

33 whatenlightenment.net, posted April 22, 2009

on my mental state that I felt that I might break down completely. In desperation, I offered everything I had to Andrew: an inheritance of $80,000 that I had recently received following my father's death. As soon as I'd conveyed this offer to Andrew's office, I regretted having done so, and when no response was forthcoming I was silently relieved. A while later, however, I received a call instructing me to send the money.

This "donation" sat very badly with me, and two years after leaving Andrew's community, I demanded its return. After considerable legal wrangling, I did get my money back — an unprecedented event in Andrew Cohen's community. But there was a gag order attached; the return of my money was conditional on my willingness to sign an agreement not to publicly discuss Andrew Cohen for five years — until Independence Day, July 4th, 2008.

5

THE END

B Y mid 1999, the scales were beginning to fall from my eyes. I didn't realize it at the time, but the period of personal growth and productivity that had sustained me for so long and allowed me to feel so invested in Andrew's community and mission was coming to an end. I was about to reckon with the contradictions embodied by our community and our teacher and with my own confused, compromised and compartmentalized morality. I was about to wake up to the reality of the life I was living.

By that summer, when we arrived in a small town near Cannes, France, for Andrew's annual retreat, I had begun to feel the chill of his displeasure. A series of perceived slights and transgressions had rankled Andrew earlier that season — in particular, my failure to congratulate him for a recently published book, and my interest in a certain female student. One evening following a group meditation, I was admonished for speaking too casually to Andrew. As a member of his inner circle, I had often been on a more informal basis with him than many other students, but this small reprimand came as a signal that my status was changing.

The retreat concluded without further incident, but several days later, on a working holiday with about ten students in the south of France, Andrew casually revealed to a group of four close male students a deeply personal story that I had told him in confidence. Andrew frequently revealed information shared with him in confidence, particularly delicate information about the sex lives of community members. It is a measure of the security I'd felt with Andrew and with my position in his organization that I hadn't thought this would happen to me, so I was mortified when he revealed that I had twice in my life paid for sex. "Bill had a good time there in the Caribbean once," he said. I was forced to admit to what I had done during my vacation some twenty years prior.

But my embarrassed admission was not the end of it. I was urged to elaborate on the experience rather than hide from the truth of it. When I did, I was accused of being too revealing, too indulgent of salacious details. Gradually, the indictment of a questionable act became an indictment of my sexuality. Andrew would say, "Bill has a sexual issue," leaving fellow students—and even me—to wonder what he meant. I felt bewildered, belittled and angry. I had submitted to Andrew's intrusions into my private life. I had allowed him to dictate the parameters of my romantic attachments. I had abided by his rules and regulations and, in so doing, denied myself a full sexual life. Now, I was being judged harshly by him and by my peers.

Andrew convened several meetings of these four male students with me on the subject of my sexuality, and I approached them with dread. Men I considered my brothers became adversaries. They shouted in my face, chided me, insulted me and abused me verbally. They accused me of resisting my Master and of ruining his vacation. They enumerated the ways in which I was disgusting. Each meeting was more intense and disturbing than the preceding one.

After the third meeting, I fled the villa on foot, rage pulsing through me. It was the first time in eleven years that I had considered Andrew Cohen, my Master, to be completely wrong. At night, I wandered outside in the darkness for hours. Eventually, at the edge of a field, I found a canvas bag that was clasped shut. Curious, I pried it open and discovered a putrefying deer head. I wondered if it was an omen about the soul-killing journey I now suddenly found myself on. I panicked and returned to the villa, where a fellow student found me in my room and slapped me in the face. She didn't have to tell me that the blow was from Andrew.

Around the World in 100 Days

At the end of our stay in the south of France, Andrew forbade my return to Foxhollow, ordering me, instead, to go to London. I felt dislocated, humiliated, intimidated and guilt-ridden. After having been a devoted follower and dedicated servant for so many years, I felt disoriented and abandoned once stripped of my roles and responsibilities. In London, I had none.

I behaved like a jilted lover—pouting, raging—and sending expensive bouquets with letters of apology to Andrew. I sent gifts to the woman who had been my co-leader at Foxhollow and had since taken over my job. I sent her a $500 gift certificate to Saks Fifth Avenue. I persisted, sending flowers, letters and expensive shirts to Andrew. When another community member, likely at Andrew's insistence, slapped me in the face, I thanked him, despite the anger I struggled to conceal.

As my situation and state of mind deteriorated, I decided to write to Andrew and offer him the last remnant of my self-worth—which is to say, my net worth. It had worked for other students in the past. When Andrew determined that a student had failed in some particularly egregious way, that student had to "buy" his forgiveness by making a large donation. In the twisted reality in which I found myself, I considered this my last, best option. I did not think, *"Leave this community."* I did not seek to reclaim my dignity. Instead, I blamed myself for my nightmarish reversal of fortune, and I wrote to Andrew as a supplicant to his Master. I told him that I wanted to surrender all that I had so that I could be pure and worthy of his grace. What I wanted to give up was everything that seemed in any way to be mine: my $80,000 inheritance. For good measure, I threw in my car and my sex life, vowing celibacy for a decade. Money and sex—I offered to relinquish both in the name of love for my guru.

Weeks passed until a response came from Foxhollow: I was to move at once to Australia to join another penitent there. My crime: "Betraying Andrew and his Teachings." I was told that if I didn't "come through," I would never see Andrew again. Despite the expense, and the lack of notice, I left that night. I was coming undone mentally and emotionally. Fortunately, Australia gave me room to breathe. I exhaled for the first time since the trauma of France. And then, just as precipitously, Andrew ordered me to return to Foxhollow. I had been in Australia for only six days.

In Boston a few days later, I was told to await further instructions. After several nights in a hotel, I finally received word that I was to move into the student house in Cambridge, where, just as I had during my first days following Andrew, I was to share a room with several men. My mortification deepened with each day and its attendant indignities. Community members—some of whom were much younger than me and just starting out on their paths with Andrew—insulted me. I also had to contend with the painful realization that I had fallen very far and had done so very publicly within the community.

Then came a lavish floral bouquet with a card that read, "Dear Bill, sorry you're having a hard time. Love, Andrew." I snapped. In panic and rage, I grabbed my few belongings and sped off in my car. But remorse and fear of the consequences trailed me, and it was not long before I was back at the Cambridge house, enduring confrontational meetings that had my character flaws as their focus.

Something in me shifted. Though still in a fog, I no longer cared in the same way I once had. Sometime thereafter, word came from Andrew's office at Foxhollow: I was to send the $80,000 that I had pledged. Despite regretting having made the offer, I still wanted redemption. With great reluctance, I sent the check. I borrowed $10,000 of it, thus joining the ranks of so many of Andrew's followers who were in debt because of their "donations."

Not long after I sent Andrew the money, I learned that a colleague of mine had fled the London community and was in Rotterdam. Because of the atmosphere of fear and intimidation in Andrew's communities, students who wanted to leave often chose to do so surreptitiously during the night. My colleague had done so despite having been threatened with physical harm by another student, a martial arts specialist, should he attempt such an escape. In a conversation with Andrew's assistant, I remarked casually that I felt inclined to look for the escapee and bring him back. The next thing I knew, I was en route to Rotterdam. It was a mission on Andrew's behalf, I told myself, and I felt relief at having been chosen for it. Quite by chance, I did find the student there, but there was no convincing him to return to London. I had failed, but at least I had tried, and that seemed to have improved my lot when I returned once more to Cambridge.

I attended the annual New Year's retreat in Rishikesh, India, which came and went without incident—a considerable relief to me. By the time I returned to America in June of 2000, after having remained in India for an additional three months scouting locations for an Indian center, I felt I was on somewhat surer footing.

I was allowed back to Foxhollow. Though no longer a leader in the community, I jumped back into work and life there, bolstered by what seemed to be the community's forgiveness. I began each day at 3 A.M. with a three-hour practice of one thousand prostrations before a photograph of Andrew. Then I meditated for two hours and began my workday at 9 A.M. At men's meetings, I was wary of provoking the ire I had sparked in the past. I didn't, but neither did I gain insight into how or why I had so precipitously fallen out of favor. Suddenly, I was back in the realm—or at least it seemed to me that I was. In fact, however, this respite from the previous year's abuse and inhumane treatment was to be relatively brief, and my days in Andrew's community were numbered. In the meantime, though, despite my churning doubt, I felt renewed confidence and was joyful to be with my close friends again, while realizing at the same time that I could no longer fully trust that these aspects of my community life were "for real."

One day, Andrew called me into his office and told me that he wanted me to search for a new property for his London Center. I took on the assignment with zeal, never thinking for very long about whether my donation had bought me better treatment and renewed responsibility. I felt committed to my guru. Over the next several months, I found an appropriate property in London's Islington district and helped to arrange for its purchase.

Then, as if with the flick of a switch, I was back on the outside. I was evicted from my quarters in a student house in London and sent to share two small rooms with two men and a woman, the four of us having been identified as "having a problem." My boomerang existence had resumed, and it continued for the next several months, until I was told to return to Massachusetts to live with two other fallen male students.

During that nightmare period, as I struggled to regain my sense of dignity and self-worth, I delved into Nelson Mandela's autobiography. That he had managed to preserve his dignity in the face of such suffering inspired me. Of course, no one had jailed me; I had imprisoned myself and had submitted willingly to inhumane treatment. Still, Mandela's writings buoyed me during a critical time and helped me summon the courage I needed to win back my freedom.

Now I was really running on empty, and whatever conviction I had left was not enough to sustain me. Attempts to regain Andrew's good favor having proved futile, I and my fellow exiled students made one final bid for his forgiveness: Over two nights, we performed prostrations from Lenox to Foxhollow, a distance of about three miles. I felt deep exhaustion and scant devotion. Some days later, I was summoned back to Foxhollow and told, once again, that I was no longer welcome there. I felt nothing. Not yet. Not even relief. I decided to leave the community for good.

The Summit Motel sits high in the Berkshire Mountains in the tiny town of Florida, Massachusetts. That is where I spent the first two days of my new life. From my window, I could see for miles. I was aware that something very important was happening. In the days following my departure from Foxhollow and from Andrew Cohen's world, I began to feel joy and liberation. I had anticipated that I might feel overcome with guilt or shame. Instead, I felt gratitude—to myself. I was back; my life had been returned to me. Autonomy, individuality, freedom—all of the precious things

I had been conditioned to live without—were once again mine. These words of Nietzsche really capture my feelings at that time: "At long last the horizon appears free to us again, even if it should not be bright; at long last our ship may venture out again, venture out to face any danger; all the daring of the lover of knowledge is permitted again; the sea, *our* sea, lies open again: perhaps there has never been such an 'open sea.'"[34]

---

34 Nietzsche, Friedrich, *The Gay Science*, New York: Vintage Books, 1974, p. 343

6

THE SPIRITUAL LIFE

If the spiritual teacher or spiritual master is authentic, they should be able to embody and manifest the kind of humility that proves or demonstrates, for people that have eyes to see, that they are on bended knee more than anyone else, so to speak, because of their recognition of spirit's true face.... Many [of my students] were shocked when they found out that their personal relationship to me was in the end irrelevant if the truth of our relationship, or what it was really based on, didn't come first...but if that doesn't come first, then our friendship is actually inhibiting the truth of who I am and the truth of what their own potential is, and inhibits the potential of our relationship to empower both of us and to enlighten the world.... The greatest gift we can bring to the world is a vessel for spirit, because the more vessels for spirit there are, the more spirit comes into the world, and then we're doing the greatest good. So when a truly enlightened teacher sees all the individuals who come to them as potential vehicles for spirit, and doesn't really care so such about...the predicament of the particular individual...suddenly [we] realize that what we believe is the most important part of ourselves—our sense of being an individual, our sense of being special, our sense of being unique—[is] not what's really important here, but [whether you are] capable of humbling yourself enough so that spirit will be able to move through you as it moves through me.

–Andrew Cohen[35]

I T can be a life-altering experience to meet a powerful and charismatic guru. Bliss, surrender, revelation; with the decision to follow a spiritual leader comes a powerful swirl of sensations. In order to believe in the guru, one must have the experience of something authentic, as I did. One may feel that a certain quality has been transmitted, what some might call a

35 "The Teacher-Student Relationship: Genpo Roshi & Andrew Cohen," youtube.com, posted June 29, 2009

"spiritual experience." In the Eastern traditions, there is a deeper understanding of such phenomena, referred to in various esoteric disciplines — including Orthodox Christianity — as *illuminatio, shaktipat, kensho,* or *kundalini awakening.* Of the many people who chose to follow Andrew Cohen over the years, those who did not feel his particular spiritual transmission did not remain in his community for long. Among those who did experience something profound, many devoted years of their lives to Andrew's mission and his communal paradigm; I, for example, spent thirteen years as a devotee. For myself and for others like me, Andrew's magnetism emboldened us to abandon the familiar. Leaving home, friends and family, while it looked crazy from the outside, was possible only because we felt deeply that a new social network of profounder allure awaited us.

The guru/disciple bond is a powerful one that is little understood by those who have not experienced it for themselves, and today it is a relatively rare individual who willingly cedes his or her autonomy to another with neither a guarantee of protection nor the support or blessing of family and friends. It is as life-altering a decision as joining the military or embarking on missionary work abroad, but there is no celebratory *bon voyage* party for the individual on a spiritual quest. He or she goes it alone, as I and many others did.

While one can comprehend what turns the casual follower into a devotee, it is perhaps harder to understand why an intelligent, thinking adult *remains* devoted once the quality of the experience with the guru has begun to deteriorate or, as in my case, has been marred by humiliation and abuse. In order to endure such harsh circumstances for extended periods, there must be something else at play — namely, an open heart. This is difficult to understand if one has not experienced it firsthand. The guru's social context and his attendant community have become the new follower's friends and family. Bonds formed in such a environment can, for some followers, be stronger than any previous and are consequently very difficult to break — even beyond a point at which continued membership in the community has become harmful to one's self and sense of self.

PROPHETIC CHARISMA

We are fortunate to have the work of Len Oakes, a psychologist who has studied charismatic groups and cults extensively, using a methodology that has enabled him to incorporate both an insider's and an outsider's perspective. Uniquely situated as a former member of one such group who was permitted by its leader to return as an objective researcher, Oakes has documented his findings in a groundbreaking book, *Prophetic Charisma: The Psychology of Revolutionary Religious Personalities,* in which he charts, among the many groups considered in his study, what turns out to be the relatively common trajectory of the charismatic leader's early development and later career. Oakes also examines the factors that both draw followers into the leader's orbit and ultimately cause the majority of them to leave it. Exploring the process through which the student becomes bound to the teacher, Oakes sheds light on the particular qualities that make possible the guru/disciple relationship in the first place, identifying four elements crucial to the formation of this unique bond:

Faith – The student deeply believes in the existence of some individual who can guide and support the quest to learn and manifest the ultimate meaning of life.

Trust – The student trusts the guru inherently and so confides in him his deepest hopes and fears. His willingness to do so represents a posture of extreme vulnerability hinging on a kind of guru/disciple honor system – i.e., the student reveals all and the teacher, far from abusing this information, uses it only for the skillful dismantling of the student's ego. For the student, the potential for universal reward – freedom from conditioning and inner limitation in the service of humanity – trumps the possibility of betrayal.

Courage – The guru embodies for the disciple such elusive qualities as inner freedom, independence from convention, and profound calm and confidence. In order to accomplish what Oakes calls the disciple's "great work" — his most important creative project or ultimate concern — the follower summons his own deepest courage while looking to the guru's perceived accomplishments and qualities for inspiration.

Projection — The follower projects ideal qualities onto the leader, such as saintliness or godliness. Precisely because of the self-confidence the guru projects, it is possible for the follower to become absolutely convinced of the leader's purity and transcendence. Without projection and the idealization that flows from it, there would be very little to hold one to a merely human — i.e., flawed (and possibly abusive) — guru.[36]

As noted earlier, it is important to understand that some or all of these elements also characterize student/teacher relationships in several institutionalized esoteric traditions of long standing, and I leave open the question of whether the dynamics described here represent a boon or a danger in contexts more traditional than new religious movements such as Andrew Cohen's.

With his or her "great work" within reach, confidence blooms in the new follower. The result can be an unprecedented period of focused work and productivity, underscored and fortified by devotion to the guru. My own such experience galvanized my ardor for Andrew Cohen, his teachings and his community, and kept me going for a number of years. I dove into community life, meditation and other spiritual practices. My "great work" became the search for, negotiation of the purchase of, and eventual co-direction of the property that became EnlightenNext's world headquarters. It was an exhilarating time, as the spiritual seeker's "great work" period is apt to be. Unfortunately, however, the experiences of this period *were not grounded in reality*. Cracks began to appear in the façade as I realized the extent of the divide between the Andrew Cohen I'd come to idealize and the individual I actually saw. This, according to Oakes, is a common occurrence;

---

36 Oakes, Len, *Prophetic Charisma: The Psychology of Revolutionary Religious Personalities*, Syracuse, NY: Syracuse University Press, 1997, pp. 127-129

and for many followers, once reality begins to dawn, as it had for me, there is no going back to the illusion.

Reckoning with the reality of the situation not only casts the guru into sharp focus, it also forces deep self-examination in the disciple. Often, the result is the painful awareness that the initial spiritual experience, whatever positive effects it may have had, has also fed the vein of a longstanding psychological neurosis — and that the two have, unfortunately, become entwined. This neurosis takes the form of a feeling of unworthiness from which only association with a Great Person can redeem one by activating an environment or field in which it is possible to acknowledge and transcend one's faults. In this way, the self-affirming quest for spiritual fulfillment has taken a detour into self-destructive neurotic codependency. The student's yearning for spiritual guidance and the teacher's need for adoration have locked both into an unhealthy and potentially dangerous cycle of dominance and submission, and neither the guru nor the disciple can be truly free so long as they continue to be driven by these entangled motivations.

Most students' journeys, according to Oakes, go something like this: an inspired beginning, characterized by a profound experience of freedom, bliss and bonding with the guru; the identification and pursuit of the "great work"; followed eventually by façade-crumbling revelations concerning the underlying exploitation of needs that has also been taking place. It is a journey, in short, from idealism to disappointment.

It is a fact that the career trajectories of many charismatic leaders end in sudden freefall — a steady climb followed by a dire and precipitous drop — and the *visible* culprit is corruption. While there has been much debate about whether this corruption is the inevitable result of a skewed power dynamic such as characterizes the guru/disciple relationship, corruption of one sort or another is clearly so prevalent in many new religious communities that it seems reasonable to ask whether this potential for abuse is intrinsic to any system of authoritarian power, or is merely a seed — a latent potential—preexisting in the personalities of only certain leaders. Either way, a person with a deep psychological need to be "The One" might turn out to be anointed, self-appointed or both. In Andrew's case, his guru had asserted that he, Andrew, was destined to lead many people to "enlightenment." Should this have led necessarily to corruption? Did it? (It is a telling manifestation of the dynamic we are addressing here that, according to recent testimony by some of Andrew Cohen's remaining long-term students, not so much as a hint of corruption, in Cohen's community, has ever existed.)[37]

According to my observation, corruption occurs if and when the leader's escalating need for affirmation exceeds the amount he actually receives. Followers, after all, are ordinary mortals, with all of the flaws that ordinary mortals have, and can't always live up to the guru's requirements and expectations. For the guru who seeks total adoration and absolute control, the merely human student represents more than disappointment or failure; he represents a volitional affront that is intolerable to the extreme "spiritual sensitivity" supposedly embodied by the guru. And once the guru descends to coercion to get what he wants from his students—whether it be adulation, obedience or money—he may find himself inclined to use a little more each time, until coercion becomes abuse and abuse becomes a default response endemic to his system as a whole. The result is corruption, which ultimately erodes the guru's leadership and his students' belief in him, leading to his downfall.

THE AUTHORITARIAN DYNAMIC

But let's be honest: The guru's authority isn't foisted upon the unsuspecting. It is *sought*, and acceptance as a student represents not only an affirmation of one's highest ideals but also a personal affirmation—just as, for the guru, the high regard of stu-

---

37 "Our Experiment to Create a New Unity in Consciousness and Culture—The Inside Story of EnlightenNext's Evolution," posted April 24, 2009 (UK archive), enlightennext. org/webcast

   "Andrew Cohen and the Birth of an Evolutionary and Integral Teaching," posted May 7, 2009 (US archive), enlightennext.org/webcast

dents (and especially of many students) represents a validation of his role that is both institutional and personal. In other words, the guru/disciple relationship is not one-sided, and in practical terms its initiation changes the student's life in a fundamental way by conferring on him or her a *position* within the community, which in turn confers at least some degree of *proximity to the guru*. In some cases, such as mine, that proximity progressed to membership on the EnlightenNext (at that time "Impersonal Enlightenment Fellowship") Board of Directors, and included other leadership positions along the way, many involving extensive travel between centers and teaching venues. It can be intoxicating to be recognized for one's demonstrated commitment—and conversely, it can hurt very much not to be. It is according to the guru's whim alone that a given student receives or loses the favor of his attention; thus, the student's devotion is offered with a twinge of self-doubt and always engenders a fear of possible inadequacy.

At the same time, the authoritarian leader knows that when some are favored and others are not, the effect can be destabilizing to the community as a whole, and he both tempers his whims according to this recognition and exploits it. His fire and magnetism keep things churning, attracting new followers and breathing life into the communal structures already in place. But his seemingly unquenchable need for more—more recognition, more devotion, more followers, more success, more tangible change, more enlightenment, and, yes, more money—eventually undermines his work and his potential to do good. His narcissism—his need to be "The One"—prevents him from seeing his own flaws, and he comes to believe with increasing fervor that he is morally unassailable and beyond human reproach. In time, as his delusional self-righteousness grows, his project becomes toxic and dangerous; consider that Da Free John, Baghwan Shree Rajneesh, Swami Muktananda, Yogi Amrit Desai and Andrew Cohen have each repeatedly faced serious allegations of physical, emotional and financial abuse.

According to Oakes's analysis, there are five stages in the development of a charismatic authoritarian's sense of his own prophetic vocation:

Early narcissism – As a child he is given to believe, intentionally or circumstantially, that he is inordinately special.

Incubation – Seeking to establish a role appropriate to his uniqueness, he locates in everyday occurrences and experiences of adversity symbols of his "specialness and proof of his calling."

Awakening – An enlightenment experience, or some other perceived affirmation from God that he has been singled out for this great calling; Andrew Cohen "received" his "awakening" from his guru, Poonja (whom he only later renounced as himself corrupt and compromised).

Mission – The task that follows his "awakening"; imbued with a sense of being the "sole source of ultimate good for others," the guru becomes a full-fledged "prophet" and seeks to lead his own flock.

Decline or fall – The final stage, possibly preordained by the prophet's narcissism-driven unreality.[38]

THE DEVOTEE'S DEPARTURE

The guru becomes more brittle over time. His sense of grandeur and self-importance is not reflected back to him by the world, and this creates conflict without and anxiety within. His students leave, but the guru never considers himself the probable cause; rather, their departures prove his contention that he alone has what it takes to live according to his teachings, and that anyone who leaves is a failure. Of 130 of Andrew Cohen's original students, 123 have left him, and Cohen has vilified almost all of them for having done so. (In those rare instances when he publicly "wishes someone well," he usually has calculated political

---

38 Oakes, *op. cit.*, pp. 42-43

reasons for doing so.)[39] Cohen has also invented a term for the far-flung community of his former followers: the "shadow *sangha*." In his online essay, "A Declaration of Integrity," Cohen invokes a subtle and challenging "spiritual context" to defend himself against these critics, while deriding them as "a small group of disgruntled former students" who have "failed miserably" at the spiritual life and who are driven by bitterness and a sense of personal failure.[40]

Cohen seems to be obsessed with his former students and their criticism of him, and though this is understandable in light of their potential to reveal his most closely guarded secrets, his dismissive attitude offers them little incentive to respect or protect him. For students inside Andrew's community, however, his obsession with those who leave helps to create an impenetrable wall around the *ashram*. The subject of leaving is not discussed openly, unless the direction of the conversation is the condemnation of one who has left. As a result, many followers are so afraid to leave that they do so only under cover of darkness, like refugees fearing reprisal; and in that act of leaving, the individual is entirely alone, foregoing all previous companionship and support. Within the community, a departure is treated like a death in the family that is not to be discussed. It is as though the person never existed. Such was the case with a wonderful and much-loved man, Jerry Paup, who left Andrew's community in the 1990s. A few years after having left, Jerry died; some of his old friends in the community did not learn of his passing until years later.

Andrew Cohen's diatribes about leaving are intimidating. He often predicts eternal damnation or the total evaporation of one's spiritual life — the rest of one's days given over to the dull, meaningless grind of *samsara*, the illusory world outside the arena

---

39 Two examples come to mind. One is Jane O'Neil, the donor of the $2,000,000 that financed the purchase of Foxhollow. Cohen's proxy writes: "Ms. O'Neil was a close student for some time and a friend to many at EnlightenNext. We still have warm feelings towards her and greatly appreciate what her generosity made possible. EnlightenNext wishes her well and hopes she has continued success in her chosen path." (See *Chapter 14*.) The other is Craig Hamilton, former Managing Editor of Cohen's magazine, *EnlightenNext*, whose biography and media contacts (posted on the magazine's website) underscore the strategic importance of maintaining cordial relations.
40 "A Declaration of Integrity," andrewcohen.org/blog, posted October 18, 2006

of total commitment and dedication to "truth" and "evolution." Often, a follower who has been in the community for a number of years, after secretly contemplating leaving, will decide to stay, or to defer temporarily a final decision—even when faced with disturbing uncertainty, or the grim prospect of a degree of rage and abuse on Cohen's part possibly greater than any previously experienced. One might think, *"I've already given eight years. How can I leave now?"* and choose to throw oneself back into the life of the community with greater surrender and abandon in the hope that things will improve. But since in the end all but a few will choose not to spend the rest of their lives in the group, the act of leaving the guru is as common—and as significant—as the decision to follow him.

GRIEVING

The decision to leave signals the death of a dream, and as with the death of a loved one, the realization that one's hopes have turned to ashes can trigger tremendous grief. One also faces the challenge of reasserting one's independence in the world after having lived for so long according to the rules and expectations of another. For some, there is also the challenge of rediscovering one's own self-worth after enduring the humiliations and abuses of a particularly degrading way of life. For others, grief is replaced by a steely determination to make up for lost time. For all who leave, it seems to be necessary to return to what preceded the guru experience, and to tap back into those activities that one once considered beautiful, promising and uplifting. But even so, those who leave cannot avoid feelings of tremendous loss. Leaving a guru is a divorce of sorts, and leaving a community is like leaving behind a family. It is a separation from a place of living, from activities and pastimes, from social conventions and in some cases manners of dress, diet and ways of relating. Everything is uprooted. It is traumatic. It causes grief. And it may take years to come to terms with it.

Some find themselves working through the trauma on a sub-conscious level. I have had dreams about being back in the community; in fact, I had this dream several times a week for several years. In the dream, I was back, didn't want to be there, and was trying to plan my escape. Everyone was glad to see me, but no one knew how much I wanted to leave. I have that dream much more rarely now, but I still have it. My dream is about loss and separation—the loss of friends, a mooring, a spiritual direction—and the ambivalence that I feel about it all.

Very few regret leaving, even if life afterward is difficult, but the relative success of the healing process depends on what comes next, and it seems to be important to reintegrate oneself into the "ordinary" world, and to find meaning in one's daily life, in order truly to heal. And what happens, in the meantime, to one's attraction to higher values—to love, to truth—that inspired one's spiritual quest in the first place? The short answer: It doesn't go away.

It was a deep spiritual longing that inspired one to drop everything in the first place, and once one is back in a settled life with commitments, possibly a partner, a new job and new friends, one may begin to realize that the spiritual search does not necessarily require a teacher—not, at least, in the old authoritarian way. One looks around and considers the alternatives, whether reengaging with formal spiritual practice or going for solitary walks, and many questions remain. What about enlightenment, about spiritual authenticity? How authentic was the guru, how nurturing and supportive of his followers' commitment to him and the pursuit of their "great work"? What was the source of the depth of love and spiritual fire that one experienced? Was it due to the guru's grace, or to the sincerity and fire of those who had gathered around him?

The spiritual longing that first brought one to the charismatic or authoritarian guru is still present, even if it is now buried beneath the memory of many harsh and difficult experiences. What is helpful is to try to understand what happened, to find a way out of self-blame, and to realize how broad the path of spiritual authenticity actually is. One recovers some measure of dignity and maturity in the process of this reckoning — an unexpected and unintended gift of the years spent with one's "teacher."

7

WOMEN AND ENLIGHTENMENT

No exploration of the dynamic between Andrew Cohen and his students would be complete without a closer look at his treatment of women. Like many others in his community, I observed that he drew a distinction between his male and female students. At first, these distinctions seemed benign, and his ultimate emphasis was ostensibly on "liberation without a face," i.e., freedom from the compulsive need to emphasize or identify with one's gender-based characteristics. Over time, however, because Andrew claimed to be a "unique teacher with regard to the liberation of women," women in his community were subjected to enormous pressure from him to conform to this ideal by transcending what he referred to as "the women's conditioning."

It was my personal observation over the course of my thirteen years as Andrew's student that he either regarded women as second-class citizens or harbored some hidden resentment toward them, and that, because of this unacknowledged bias, women were subjected to humiliations that exceeded even those which many of the men had to endure. The following post from the whatenlightenment.net blog offers a revealing picture of the kind of treatment to which women as a group were subjected in his community.

Andrew did have some powerful insights into the challenges that women face on the spiritual path and typical features of "women's conditioning." However, these are insights that just about anyone would come to if they looked into it. One *major* problem with Andrew's approach is that he reified the "woman's ego," making it into a kind of larger-than-life monster to fight with. However, this was his approach to dealing with the ego in general—a very dualistic approach, doomed to failure.

Andrew constantly berated and shamed individual women and groups of women for expressing "women's ego" or "women's conditioning." All kinds of expressions of fear, hesitation, self-concern, rebelliousness, impatience, pride, jealousy, failure to surrender, resistance, wanting to stay in control, etc. (the typical human stuff), became not just challenges that human beings were dealing with on the spiritual path but *women's treachery*. Although he asserted that he believed that women could transcend their deep conditioning as women, he often said that women by their very nature undermine the *dharma* (echoing an early Buddhist scripture) and have a deep and possibly insurmountable resistance to enlightenment. He often accused women of trying to destroy him and his teachings, of trying to "quell" his "revolution."

All of this is what was illustrated in the women's sauna at Foxhollow…the walls of [which] were covered with blown-up messages from Andrew, letters to him from women, passages from texts, and huge cartoons depicting women acting out the horrors of the "women's condition," including images of specific women in the community gleefully pulling out Andrew's entrails, burning his books, and engaging in sadomasochistic acts. A video of the films *To Die For* and *Black Widow* and a recording of Bob Dylan's "Just Like a Woman" were to be kept running 24/7. Spatters of red paint symbolized Andrew's blood that the women were spilling.

The "context" of all of this is what I described above—Andrew trying to liberate women through forcing them to face the truth about themselves ("The truth will set you free"). We were required to spend an hour a day in the sauna, and ideally more, reading and reflecting on its contents as part of our daily spiritual practice. I find this to be one of Andrew's most bizarre "teaching" gestures. I doubt if it helped anyone; I certainly think it did more harm than good.

In the context I've just described, Andrew saw himself (and perhaps still does) as the first and only true liberator of women because he is willing to help women—and force them if necessary—to face this truth about themselves. Motivated by this vision of himself as a liberator of women, he subjected individual women, and especially, groups of women, to many extreme exercises in "facing the truth" about themselves. These included treating the women as pariahs, the lake episode[41], and having them recount and record together over the course of many days all of the ways in which they had acted over the years in ways that "quelled the revolution."

The women were given a *mantra* to recite for forty-five minutes or an hour a day, something like, "The liberation of women solely depends on my unconditional willingness to surrender my compulsive need to relate to each and every thought, feeling, experience, and event as a vehicle for my own reflection." (There is some insight here into the *human* tendency to self-reference, but another very ham-handed and ego-reifying approach to the phenomenon.) And during long stretches of time, there were relentless series of hours-long meetings (often lasting almost all night, with women struggling to make do on almost no sleep) that were far worse than the most extreme encounter groups of the 1970s, with Andrew sending messages to the group about their "betrayal." There were also numerous retreats that were like 24/7 encounter groups that went on for a week, with numerous women simply breaking down and many women leaving the community altogether.

At the same time, groups of men also would occasionally come under similar pressure. On the whole, however, I would say that Andrew's treatment of women was consistently more extreme, and characterized by his particular convictions about women.[42]

Obviously, then, I am not alone in my observation that women in Andrew Cohen's community were at a disadvantage by virtue of their gender. In the essays that follow, three other former members of the EnlightenNext community share their reflections, recollections and observations about Andrew Cohen's treatment of women.

41 See *Chapter 3.*
42 whatenlightenment.net, posted April 22, 2009

THE WOMEN'S CONDITIONING
Andre Van der Braak

Andrew always struck me as skeptical of women's abilities to live his teachings. In 1989, he started to talk about a deeply rooted resistance in women that was not present in men. In 1992, he began to espouse a theory about "women's conditioning." According to Andrew, millennia of deeply rooted conditioning have engrained in women a survival instinct that prevents them from truly letting go of what is personal. It is Andrew's contention that women, so rooted in personal experience, are incapable of embracing the impersonal perspective.

It is my opinion that Andrew considers his female students inferior to his male students. In 1997, Andrew started to put increasing pressure on the women to be more objective, less emotional and less personal. The catalyst for this seemed to be strife with his wife, Alka, who Andrew felt was not surrendering to him. At a retreat with Alka and several other senior women students, Andrew addressed what he called the women's craving of affirmation from men and asserted that as women they were more interested in affirmation than in truth. He charged that women use what they're good at — sex and service, according to Andrew — to buy men off so that they don't have to face themselves.

Andrew's focus on women's conditioning became a central issue. His pressure on the women peaked during the retreat in Rishikesh in 1998. There, Andrew explained that when he began to teach, he believed that women have an easier time than men on the spiritual path by virtue of their ability to be in touch with their feelings, to exhibit ecstasy without feeling shame, to surrender, and to love deeply. "But I've found over the years," Andrew said, cackling, "that when they're challenged to allow real intimacy beyond feelings, beyond emotional devotion, women respond with a big NO!"

Andrew's voice rose as he explained that he felt a "No!" rising up in his meetings with the *sangha* women. He described it as a wall of fear and aggression that he did not know the origin of and did not understand. Whereas Andrew had once thought that women had less ego and more generosity, he now said, "I've found out that that's where their ego hides, that's where it takes refuge."

As Andrew paused, my thoughts drifted to an incident that had taken place the previous night. Clara, one of Andrew's long-time students, had complained about the heavy work schedule in the kitchen and the absence of free time. Andrew became furious when he heard about it. "I know her," he shouted. "She's always whining!" He ordered the other women to throw Clara's bedding and her personal belongings out the window. When Clara returned from her kitchen shift that night, she found that she was homeless.

The uncomfortable silence in the room deepened as Andrew continued his talk. Speaking in an almost hushed tone, Andrew said, "For women, it's a lot harder to come together, it's a lot harder to trust. Their ego is more insidious. They can be friends on a personal level and be very open with each other, but coming together in an impersonal way — they don't want to touch that with a ten-foot pole! They become competitive and mean to each other and rip each other to pieces!"

Again, my thoughts drifted. A few days earlier, Andrew had ordered all the women students to bathe in the cold Ganges as a ritual of repentance. One of the women was suffering from a concussion. She explained to the *sangha* doctor that the immersion might be dangerous given her condition, but she was still required to participate. As I considered this episode, I asked myself, *"Is this what impersonality means? Nothing is personal, therefore no concern for individual feelings is necessary? Everyone is fair game since we're only shooting at the ego, not at each other?"* I tried to chase away my doubt by telling myself that the matter of the concussion may have been exaggerated.

Meanwhile, one of the men in the group challenged Andrew. "But aren't men much more competitive than women?" he asked. Andrew nodded. In the world, in their work, on a superficial level, men seem more competitive, he said. But once they break through that, they can really meet. They can be really honest. Most women are never really honest with themselves and with each other. "It's too threatening," Andrew said. "They feel it would literally be the end of them."

Andrew sighed, as though facing the prospect of an impossible mission.

"I've let it go for too long," he said, "but now I'm determined to take on the women's conditioning. I want all of you [gesturing toward the women] to crush this deep-seated biological programming and [these] culturally determined ideas about what a woman is. I don't care what it takes. I mean it. It might mean that all of you run away and I end up with only men students."

Silence followed. Some of the men looked at each other with worry in their eyes. The women, crushed and not knowing what to say or do, sat with downcast eyes. Then Andrew interrupted the silence with an accusation. "I feel no response from you whatsoever," he said to the women. "I don't know what to do anymore to reach you. Why don't you all leave now and have a meeting together. I want you to come up with a response."

One by one the women exited the room. Andrew addressed the men in a confidential tone, telling us how frustrated he felt with the women and asking for our solidarity. He urged us to stand together as men in this historic fight against a deeply rooted archetypal conditioning. "No one has taken this on before," Andrew said, explaining that the women were looking for affirmation, and warning us not to be taken in by their wiles. He asked us to deny them the affirmation they craved and advised us to approach them in a strictly formal way. We were not so much as to smile at the women. We were not to give them the feeling that things were okay. We assured Andrew that we were at his side in this war against the women's conditioning.

In the course of the retreat, Andrew's measures against the women escalated. He humiliated them publicly in community meetings, ranting and yelling at them. He wanted the women to come up with a response, to make a gesture. He forbade the women to apologize on the grounds that apology is their built-in response to make things okay. When some women made the mistake of apologizing, they were banished from the retreat.

During one of the *sangha* meetings, Andrew had some of the older students sit in a circle and imitate what goes on in women's meetings. The ridicule drove the women to despair. Andrew proposed that the men sever their romantic ties with women in the community so that the women would be left to themselves. Some of the men resisted that, especially a Dutch student who had a child. We gave him a hard time for being so bourgeois. In the end, the relationships held.

Again, doubt bubbled to the surface of my psyche. *"Why is Andrew so harsh with the women?"* I asked myself. *"Could it have something to do with his difficult relationship with his mother?"* A few months before the Rishikesh retreat, Andrew's mother, Luna Tarlo, had published a book that was very critical of Andrew. In *The Mother of God*, she tells the story of her son's meeting with Poonja and his subsequent transformation into a guru. The book depicts life in Andrew's community as a kind of horror story. Andrew was furious when it came out, and spent long meetings with his students in Foxhollow deriding the book and reading aloud from it to show how utterly ridiculous and unfounded certain passages were. I wondered, *"Is Andrew projecting his anger towards his mother onto his women students?"*[43]

MEETING VIMALA, LEAVING ANDREW
Wendyl Smith

The retreat in India in 1998 marked the apex of a long period during which Andrew had bullied his women students over what he called their failures. At the end of that retreat, Andrew joined a group of women in a visit to Vimala Thakar, the spiritual heir to J. Krishnamurti, in Mt. Abu in Rajasthan. Thakar is a very beautiful, generous and wise soul who had been featured in an interview

---

43 From Van der Braak, Andre, *Enlightenment Blues: My Years with an American Guru*, Rhinebeck, NY: Monkfish Book Publishing Company, 1998

in *What is Enlightenment?* magazine at the beginning of Andrew's preoccupation with "women's conditioning."

At the time of meeting Thakar, the women were so self-conscious and flattened after that long stretch of intense berating that they could barely speak with her. Just one year earlier, before the women had become such pariahs in Andrew's community, I had joined two other formal women students in meeting Vimala. We'd had two beautiful, open, simple and profound meetings with her. In Andrew's "meeting," however, the focus was on what was "wrong" with the women. Because Andrew presided over this meeting—dominated it—the women had no collective voice. It was a pathetic encounter after which the women were harshly criticized. I say: What do you expect?

Toward the end of the retreat, to pay for our "sins," we formal women students decided to offer $750 each to Andrew for a meditation hall. A hardship for many of us, it was an insane, desperate idea put forth by one of the women in the hope that it would safeguard us from future attacks. Desperate and insane—just like the suggestion that all the women prostrate in a freezing lake in Foxhollow! There were scores and scores of insane ideas coming out of our leaden, inverted, compressed spirits.

Following the retreat, seemingly endless hours of women's meetings continued—unbearable, poisonous forums of bullying, aggression and self-fixation. The transcendent moments—and there were some—were fleeting, no match for what was a preoccupation with darkness and negativity. We attempted to pay for our "sins" by contributing money to buy expensive clothes and floral bouquets for Andrew, which had for years been the standard way to buy forgiveness. We stayed up all night writing flowery and sickening apologies to him and his lieutenants expressing our gratitude for their "wisdom."

Why did I stay? Why did I choose this? After four years in the community, I had cut myself off from friends, family and work possibilities. I was broke. I doubted myself, and I was in a mild stupor most of the time from lack of sleep. I didn't know how to fathom life outside of Andrew's community. Eventually, I began to receive cruel and nasty messages from Andrew, and it was not long before I was demoted. Andrew started the practice at this time of buying one's way back into the formal student community. I did not have the $2000 required to do this.

The atmosphere in Andrew's community is such that for the sake of their own survival, students swirl around the demoted and the fallen like hawks and vultures, alternately shunning and pecking at the wounded person. That was my experience in the wake of my demotion. Every Martha, Delores and Beth gave me her "opinion" — also known as "feedback" — about my behavior.

The inspirational message of Andrew's book, *Enlightenment is a Secret*, had resonated with me and caused my spirit to soar when I first read it in the early 1990s. I have a difficult time reconciling what I ultimately experienced in Andrew's community with what he and his writings had led me to hope I might experience. I was so dispirited during my last months in his community that, when I finally escaped in late 1998, I was in a state of deep traumatic stress for months afterwards. I would wake up every night in terror, with panic attacks and thoughts of suicide. When I left Foxhollow to be "in Hell with my family," as Andrew wrote in a message to me, I was humbled by how beautiful and generous my family was toward me, how gracious and how kind.

When I left, I read everything that I could find about the authoritarian guru phenomenon and the guru/group dynamic. Why, I wondered, do so many of us choose these situations? With the sanity and simplicity of my life now, I can hardly believe how insane and sick I became in Andrew's community. I have lived in Bali since 2001, and in my time there, I have moved out of my head and into my heart. I have fallen in love with an amazing group of young people who are a wellspring of the positive. Moved by their love, I work with them to help them find ways to support themselves. They have been a force of inspiration and change for their whole village — and for me. It is an amazing and rich adventure.

A Testosterone-fueled Enlightenment
Karen Merigo

> The spirit of the valley never dies.
> This is called the mysterious female.
> The gateway of the mysterious female
> Is called the root of heaven and earth.
> Dimly visible, it seems as if it were there,
> Yet use will never drain it.
> 　　　　　　　　—Lao Tsu, *Tao Te Ching*

When I left Andrew Cohen's community in 1996, I decided to delve into the issue of gender and spirituality in order to determine whether, as Andrew insisted, women could not possibly have a successful spiritual life. I came to this search with the conviction that my basic nature was power-hungry, manipulative and corrupt, because that is what Andrew had conditioned me to believe.

After a decade of reading, watching documentaries and listening to other spiritual figures, my conclusion is that what happened to the women in Andrew's community is proof that forty years of Women's Liberation have been no match for a collective psyche that has tolerated abuse for millennia. We were healthy, intelligent and educated women, yet after just a few years with Andrew, we had all started to believe that we were fundamentally flawed, and that our gender was to blame.

Women have a difficult time in Andrew's community because Andrew, quite simply, does not know how to deal with women. There is no doubt in my mind that Andrew initiated and incited many humiliating moments because of his conviction that deep humiliation could change a woman's nature. As his students, we participated because we believed that we were doing something truly evolutionary. We could not see at the time that, in fact, we were abetting and succumbing to a truly patriarchal view of women.

Andrew claims that he wants men and women to rise above their gender, but he wants *women* to express themselves in a way that is totally male. His "genderless enlightenment" is based on male principles. Women have a hard time connecting to his essentially male notions because our nature is different. We express ourselves differently, and that means that we express ourselves in a way that is unsatisfactory to Andrew, who cannot and does not accept our differences. Andrew views the feminine as weak. He demands that women not present their feminine selves. He fosters a notion of women's inferiority to men.

I encourage everyone — men and women — to embrace what is feminine in them and around them, even if it is not comfortable to do so. Because the feminine has been associated with what is weak in a violent society, it is time for the feminine to flex its true strength.

8

NOT FORGOTTEN –
THE STORY OF CAROLINE FRANKLYN
Mario Puljiz

I wrote this story because I felt for years that it needed to be told. For the editorial purposes of this book, the text has been amended slightly from how I published it originally but it still retains its necessary factual correctness and feel. Caroline Franklyn was Andrew Cohen's eldest formal student in London and had been his devoted disciple for seven years. No one should have to go through what she did in the final days and weeks of her life. Caroline's memory will forever be in my thoughts.

Caroline Franklyn was in her late seventies when she passed away in London in 1999. Despite her remarkable spirit, Caroline had been in delicate health for some time. Born in 1920 in the Austrian capital of Vienna, she married at seventeen and moved to Prague, where she and her husband ran a perfumery on the main Wenceslas Square. After Czechoslovakia was annexed into the German Reich in early 1939, Caroline and her husband became two of the many Jewish refugees who sought safety and freedom in England. They eventually settled in Hendon, North London.

In 1945, Caroline gave birth to a daughter and continued working with her husband to rebuild their life in exile. She ran her interior design business, raised her daughter and nursed her ailing husband for years before his death. Some time after his death, Caroline heard about J. Krishnamurti. Through studying his teachings and writings she embarked on a deep and heartfelt spiritual quest. During the 1970s and early 1980s, she regularly traveled to see "Krishnaji" teach in England and abroad. He became a source of tremendous spiritual inspiration for Caroline and was someone whom she greatly respected.

A few years after Krishnamurti's death in 1986, Caroline came across a young American teacher named Andrew Cohen. His passionate call to awaken reignited the fire in her heart. When he formed his London community in the early 1990s, Caroline became a member. She was among Andrew Cohen's first formal students in the United Kingdom. Caroline's life was constantly, thrillingly evolving. In her early seventies, she had a new and inspiring spiritual teacher and she belonged to a close-knit community of students. Perhaps most importantly, Caroline once again felt the promise of experiencing true awakening in this life.

Caroline was a bright, lively and warmhearted person who was unafraid to speak her mind, even when that meant going against the "party line" in Andrew Cohen's community. While she sometimes got things wrong or was overconfident, Caroline rarely shied away from being herself, regardless of the consequences. In a community where uniform views on a range of issues — from matters spiritual to personal, including taste in films and clothes — prevailed, Caroline had her own point of view, her own perspective. For that reason, her opinions were frequently considered unsuitable. Caroline's advanced age, despite her spirit and vitality, also set her apart. She could not always keep up with the busy and often exhausting pace in the community.

Caroline's sense of independence, strength and determination were the legacy of her extraordinary life. She left her home under life-threatening circumstances, moved to a foreign country and started a new life against the backdrop of a world war. Krishnamurti also taught her the importance of independence from religious organizations. He viewed them as obstacles, not gateways, to freedom.

Caroline never lived in Andrew Cohen's community; she remained in her townhouse in the leafy London suburb of Richmond. As such, she put herself beyond the reach of the long arm of the community. Life outside of Andrew Cohen's enclave also enabled her to maintain contact with her beloved family. Cutting off contact with one's family was one of the prices of full-time life in the community, as families were considered impediments to enlightenment. At the same time, Caroline was a devoted student of Andrew Cohen's. She regularly made a number of long weekly journeys to the community to attend meetings, events and video showings. Her family confirmed that she always spoke lovingly and with pride about her teacher and her community. They considered that Caroline's spiritual life gave her much vigor and joy that she brought to everything in her life.

The first hint of what was to come for Caroline came in January, 1998, when, during the Rishikesh retreat in India, Andrew Cohen unleashed a vitriolic attack on the formal women students in the community. He accused them of being insufficiently devoted to him, manipulative, untrustworthy and in need of a deep and complete inner change. The women were required to attend a series of meetings during which they were asked to declare their faithfulness to Andrew Cohen, confess to the charges of manipulation, and repent their sins in order to be absolved of them. Over the course of the weeks and months that followed, many of the formal female students — including Caroline — were verbally battered and emotionally broken. They were forced to step down and become lay students. Even some of us formal men students, habituated though we were to the intensity, verbal attacks and severe reprimands of such meetings, privately considered the women's meetings of that period to be too severe.

Stepping down brought a welcome, if temporary, relief to the demoted female students. It did not, however, bring about an end to their suffering. They were still forced to attend a number of weekly meetings with formal women students that Andrew Cohen considered to be in good spiritual shape. The stated aim of those meetings was to "help" the demoted women "rise up" and regain their formal student status. Forced confessions, verbal abuse and aggression were the means employed to bring about that end. Not surprisingly, Caroline — dejected, and with a health condition that often left her short of breath — never "came through" to regain her formal student status.

Many of us lost touch with Caroline after that. Such was the common but unspoken practice in the formal community: once a formal student slipped to a lower echelon, they were isolated from their former peers and paid very little mind. I later learned of Caroline's heartache over having been cruelly sidelined after so many years of deep involvement in the community. Unfortunately, to Andrew Cohen and to us, Caroline had simply become another casualty of "the war against the ego." Prevailing wisdom held that she had deserved what she had gotten.

Toward the end of 1999, Andrew Cohen came to London to conduct public teachings. For the London students, his visit presented a rare opportunity to see their teacher, who spent most of the year traveling and lecturing all over the world, in person. If one wanted to speak to him directly about one's practice, spiritual development or any other issue, his arrival in London was the time to do it. Aware of this, Caroline requested a private audience with him following a teaching on Saturday, December 11, 1999. Caroline made the request through a senior student of Andrew Cohen's who reportedly treated Caroline with contempt and refused her access to Andrew Cohen that evening. Soon after the exchange, Caroline left the teaching venue disheartened and convinced that her teacher was not going to see her.

When Caroline arrived home after the long drive back to Richmond, her phone rang. Stan Brady, another senior student of Andrew Cohen's, was calling to find out why she had not waited at the venue to see her master. Caroline recounted to Brady her discouraging exchange with the senior student, but to no avail. Brady strongly reprimanded her for having left without waiting to be seen by her teacher. Caroline protested her innocence; she believed that she had not done anything wrong. The conversation left Caroline deeply shaken and upset. She felt misunderstood, unjustly accused of having transgressed, and dismayed by Brady's rebuke.

Caroline's response clearly rankled Andrew Cohen, further confirming his conviction that she was defiant and egotistical.

The following day, Sunday, December 12, 1999, Stan Brady rang Caroline a second time. If his first attempt to pressure Caroline into "admitting her sin" had failed, he was determined that his renewed effort would not. The forty-five minute call that ensued was devastating for Caroline, who recalled that to shield herself from the intensity and volume of Brady's shouting, she had to hold the phone away from her ear. Brady told Caroline that she would "die a miserable old woman." He attacked her anew for having left the venue without waiting to see Andrew Cohen. Without regard for her physical and spiritual frailty or her humanity, Brady unleashed a vitriolic attack that left Caroline traumatized. She later said that she believed that Andrew Cohen had been present while Brady administered his tirade.

Andrew Cohen had a deep need to control all the important aspects of life in his community. Quite literally nothing of significance took place in his community without either his initiation or prior approval. Stan Brady could not have delivered such brutal feedback to Caroline without his teacher's knowledge. Rather, Brady was Andrew Cohen's surrogate, delivering precisely the message that his master wanted Caroline to hear. It is important to point out that Brady was not alone in his role as Andrew Cohen's mouthpiece; our teacher recruited many of us to relay his righteous anger to another student, to "blast" the transgressor for their egotistical tendencies. Without questioning, and persuaded that only complete obedience to Andrew Cohen would bring enlightenment, we acquiesced, accomplices to his brutality.

After the conversation had ended, Caroline Franklyn was not the same person anymore. Under Brady's enormous pressure her spirit was finally broken. She took his words to heart utterly and completely and later confided to loved ones that the experience had shattered her emotionally and had extinguished her will to live. She became consumed by intense feelings of alienation, fear and psychological torment. The way forward — in both her spiritual journey and her life — held no promise. Her health rapidly deteriorated and within days she was bedridden, a shadow of the person she had always been.

Caroline's family soon came to help, assuming that her poor health was the result of her chronic lung condition. When they learned of her traumatic telephone encounters with Stan Brady, however, they made the decision to bar Andrew Cohen's students from contact with her. They feared the consequences to Caroline's health of any further interaction with the community and sought to create a peaceful, healing environment in which to foster her recovery. Female formal students from the community called to inquire about Caroline's condition, but her family very much doubted the sincerity of their concern. They felt that the true motivation of the phone calls was purely to gather information and perform damage control on Andrew Cohen's behalf.

On December 20, 1999, Caroline was taken to the Royal Brompton Hospital in London's Chelsea district. Her health had continued to decline, and her family hoped that she would have the best chance to recover if under the care of doctors. The psychological state that Caroline was in at that time—haunted, tormented and fearful of further attacks—shocked the family to the core. They became increasingly worried that they were losing her. In their desperation, Caroline's family decided to ask through Andrew Cohen's London center if he could send a loving message to Caroline in the hope that it might bring her spirit back to life. Andrew Cohen sent a message, via a telephone call from a senior student, and his message was one of love and forgiveness. Caroline, already largely unconscious at the time that the message was relayed to her, opened her eyes for a moment upon hearing the message and her hand grip became momentarily stronger, only to weaken shortly afterwards.

Caroline Franklyn died in the Royal Brompton Hospital on December 23, 1999—only eleven days after the second phone call from Stan Brady. She was seventy-nine years old. She died with a broken heart and in a state of absolute inner terror and anguish, a wonderful and brave human spirit who had triumphed against many odds in her life but was cruelly destroyed by the very teacher and community that she had loved, trusted and devoted her spiritual life to. Caroline's family believe that she would have certainly carried on living had her spirit not been crushed to the point that she tragically gave up on life. The brave spirit that had once enabled her to triumph over pain and struggle had been broken by the very community to whom she had entrusted her love, devotion and spiritual life. Caroline's family attributes her swift decline leading to her death to the merciless attacks levied by Stan Brady on behalf of Andrew Cohen.

I was a formal student in the London community during this period, and my fellow students and I knew nothing of Caroline Franklyn's plight. The first news we had of her came in the form of a directive from Andrew: Caroline, he said, had "blown it"; none of us were to have contact with her or to discuss her situation with lower level students. We were told that Caroline had made a great mistake, that her health was now in steep decline, and that Andrew Cohen alone, with a small group of chosen formal and senior students, would be in touch with her. We did not know about Stan Brady's phone calls to Caroline or that her rapid deterioration had come in the wake of them.

When we learned of Caroline's death, we also were told that her family did not want us at her funeral. Based on our incomplete understanding of the situation, we left it at that. Some of us formal students privately felt that at least an announcement should be made to everyone that one of our own had passed away so we could come together as a community in her honor. But as our teacher initiated no such gathering and we had already been told not to get involved in anything regarding Caroline, we in the end did nothing.

I was neither alone in feeling shock about Caroline's death nor in feeling conflicted about our community's response—or lack thereof—to it. My inaction was typical of the robotic way that many formal students responded when our innate moral sense ran counter to the official position. From a perspective of obedience, the silence of the formal and senior students was the correct response; from a human point of view, however, our silence was absolutely shameful. A lay student, unaware of the gag rule on discussing Caroline Franklyn, initiated a conversation about our community's silence around her death. The student was promptly and harshly rebuked by a senior student for doing so which also ensured that any possible questioning voices in the lay community stayed silent.

The death of Caroline Franklyn was swiftly put behind and quickly forgotten. It was indeed as if Caroline had never existed — her name was rarely if ever mentioned by Andrew Cohen or his senior and formal students and the full scale of the events surrounding her death was never exposed within the community. Caroline was cremated in the Hoop Lane Crematorium in Golders Green, London. Her ashes are buried in the woodlands near Alsford in Hampshire, near the Brockwood Park Krishnamurti Center. No formal or senior students went to her funeral. The only symbol of Andrew Cohen's formal community present that day was a small wreath of white flowers. Since they had not been forbidden to attend, a few of the lay students did go to the funeral.

"Why did she have to die like that?" Caroline's daughter asked one of the lay students, struggling to grasp why her mother had to exit this world haunted and in anguish. Caroline's family later wrote a letter to Andrew Cohen to obtain explanations about the events preceding Caroline's sudden health deterioration that led to her death. He never responded.[44]

---

44 whatenlightenment.net, posted January 19, 2006

9

A LEGACY OF SCORCHED EARTH—
REFLECTIONS OF A FORMER STUDENT
Susan Bridle

I was a student of Andrew Cohen for ten years, and worked very intimately with him for many years in my work as a writer and editor for *What Is Enlightenment?* magazine and other Moksha Press publications. I have witnessed or experienced everything reported on the whatenlightenment.net blog and a great deal more. I left Andrew's community in 2001, and while I am busy with new academic, career, and spiritual goals, I am still "digesting" my experience of my relationship with Andrew and my time in his community.

Bottom line, I experienced so much that was truly profound and transformative—and that I will forever be grateful for—and also so much that was really abusive and twisted—and that still deeply saddens me. The lightest light and the darkest dark. Both. All tangled together like miles of black and white yarn entwined in a big ball at the pit of my stomach. I guess for me, I feel my work is to digest the whole thing, tease it apart, and try to come to some real maturity and wisdom about it. And without saying that Andrew doesn't have responsibility for where, in my considered opinion, he went off the rails, take responsibility for all my choices and actions, for what brought me to him, what kept me there, and what enabled me to finally move on.

One thing that continues to strike me with painful irony is that fact that Andrew would, almost tearfully, lament about other teachers who had shown such great promise, whose passion for the spiritual life and searing *dharma* inspired so many spiritual seekers to abandon "the world" and give their entire lives to a spiritual revolution—but whose abuses of sex, money, power, or other addictions in the end disillusioned thousands of seekers and instead promoted cynicism about the whole endeavor. This is, in fact, the reality of the situation now with Andrew. He inspires such passion, such commitment, such sacrifice in so many seekers…for a while, a few years, maybe ten, perhaps longer. But Andrew's legacy is, for the most part, scorched earth. Hundreds of disillusioned seekers who, when they eventually extricate themselves from their highly compromised relationship with Andrew, are scorched souls, burnt out entirely on the spiritual life, afraid to risk or trust or commit again. Many, even most, of Andrew's former students, at least those who spent significant time in his company, have lost faith in themselves, in their own aspiration and capacity, in the possibility of a healthy student/teacher relationship, in the whole enterprise. This is a crime, a sin. Worthy of a tearful lament.

When his students leave him, rather than wishing them well and hoping that they are able to make good use of their experience with him, his community, and his teachings, Andrew scorns them, heaps abuse upon them, calls them "pigs" and "monsters," and asserts that they have "sold their souls to the devil." Rather than hoping that they will go on to use what they've learned in living fruitful lives, continuing their spiritual paths, and doing good work to relieve suffering in the world, he responds gleefully when he hears news of former students who are struggling to find their way. "That loser!" he would laugh. He delighted in hearing news about struggling former students. It vindicated what Andrew saw as their personal betrayal of him, the one true living embodiment of all that is holy and evolutionary in this world. For Andrew, his game is the only real game in town; no other spiritual teacher, path, or practice can hold a candle to it. Former students' continued belief in this myth makes it very difficult for them to consider other spiritual paths and practices.

It seems that around Andrew and his communities today is a revolving door of students who discover him through the magazine or books, and have visited one of his centers, and perhaps attended a retreat or two. They stay for a while, and probably benefit tremendously. The "core" group of students who have been with Andrew for longer periods—and who are exposed to the kinds of tactics reported on the whatenlightenment.net blog—has shrunk markedly over the years. Foxhollow, Andrew's large and lavish residential and retreat center in western Massachusetts, when not filled with people during retreats and seminars, is significantly less populated than it once was. Some report that it feels like a monument to what might have been, a pretense of grandeur elaborately and expensively maintained, a slowly shriveling relic. Whether this is what becomes of Foxhollow and Andrew's worldwide spiritual community remains to be seen; Andrew's teaching and community have changed and evolved significantly since he began teaching in 1986. Maybe he will be able to adjust course regarding some of the matters discussed on the blog. That is my hope.

One other painful irony I'd like to mention—among so many others—is Andrew's early, strong criticism of "crazy wisdom" teachers. During this period, he asked Hal Blacker to interview the American spiritual teacher Lee Lozowick about it, for an article in *What Is Enlightenment?* magazine. Lozowick has enormous insight on this subject, and his comments almost seem prophetic:

WIE: *What is crazy wisdom?*

Lozowick: One of the primary aspects of crazy wisdom is that crazy-wisdom teachers are willing to use any behavior, no matter how shocking or irreverent or disturbing, if, and only if, that behavior has a very high likelihood of provoking a shift in the student, a deepening in the student. Of course, in this day and age, because of the communications industry, we hear about every idiot throughout the world whose ego takes on a crazy-wisdom function and then goes about using shock techniques whenever they feel like it, with complete disregard for the timing of the matter. Everything is timing. Gurdjieff was a master of timing. He didn't just produce shock like a research scientist to see what would happen. He only produced shock when the likelihood of its being effective, in terms of deepening a student's relationship to the Divine, was high. It didn't always work because it is only a likelihood, but still he wasn't random about it. And the teachers who I call charlatans today are teachers who are completely irresponsible in their use of power and crazy manifestation. I would consider a crazy-wisdom teacher someone who might use anything, but who is never arbitrary, and never follows their own personal motives. They only use dramatic and shocking manifestations under specific circumstances at exactly the right time. It's like faceting a diamond—if you don't understand the structure of the stone and you just take a chisel and hit it, all you get is diamond dust. You've got to know exactly the structure of the diamond because you've got to tap it along a particular fracture point. If you tap it in the middle of two fracture points, then you just smash the stone instead of getting a perfectly faceted jewel. Human beings are the same way. They've got what we could call revelation lines, so to speak, or enlightenment lines. A crazy-wisdom teacher is a master at faceting. A charlatan is someone who just takes the hammer and chisel and wails away and hopes that there are some beneficial results—or maybe doesn't even care but just loves the euphoria of the exercise of power and people groveling at his or her feet....[The fact that Reality cannot be understood with the conceptual mind] is one of the revelations that can deepen a student's relationship to the Divine. So one might do something under a specific circumstance to produce the revelation that reality is nonlinear. But ordinarily, one wouldn't function like that all the time just to prove that point. One would do that only when the student was just on the edge of the real possibility of getting that point, beyond just knowing the party line. Another important consideration is that the kind of behavior that would demonstrate the absurdity of linearity would not tend to be violent behavior or the kind of behavior that would psychologically scar someone.[45]

I think that, so sadly, Andrew became the kind of teacher Lozowick speaks about here, one "who just takes the hammer and chisel and wails away and hopes that there are some beneficial results — or maybe doesn't even care but just loves the euphoria of the exercise of power and people groveling at his or her feet."

Andrew's passion, inspiration, insight, and personal example melted my heart, and enabled me to take great risks in my commitment to the spiritual life. My association with him transformed my life in many very positive ways. I carry with me enor-

---

45 *What Is Enlightenment?* magazine, v. 20, Fall/Winter 2001

mous benefits from my time with Andrew, and I do not regret those years. But now, reflecting on his techniques, I have to say that he is an exceptionally ham-handed teacher, willing to inflict great harm in his clumsy and often extreme *dharma* experiments.

On a personal note, I'm now quite involved with the Zen Center of Denver. I've been meditating there and very slowly getting more involved for the past couple of years. I did a *sesshin* (intensive Zen retreat) last June that was very powerful. I had been afraid to do an intense retreat like that before then because I guess I felt I wasn't ready, that it would be too painful, that too much stuff around Andrew would come up. And sure enough, for the first half of the *sesshin*, layer after layer of stuff about my relationship to Andrew, to the spiritual life, to my own aspiration, to pain and cynicism came up. But I just sat with it, let it be, experienced it without clinging or pushing away. And layer by layer, it burned away like fog.

I experienced a lot of pain and grief and sadness, but also a lot of gratitude about my whole experience with Andrew. And what was also amazing was that Danan Henry Roshi, the abbot at ZCD, was at the same time coming to the end of a long process of coming to terms with his first Zen teacher, the renowned Philip Kapleau Roshi, who had died just before the sesshin.

The *sesshin* was dedicated to Kapleau Roshi, and we listened to recorded *dharma* talks by Kapleau every morning. Henry broke with Kapleau more than ten years ago, a few years after Kapleau had sanctioned him as a *dharma* heir and had sent him to open a Zen center in Denver. Henry had felt there was still something missing in his understanding, and began his Zen training all over again with Robert Aitken Roshi. (Aitken and Kapleau had both trained with the same Japanese Zen masters, but they developed very different teaching styles.) Henry's break with Kapleau was difficult for a few years, but he remained in an essentially friendly and respectful relationship with him. Nonetheless, he had a painful process of coming to terms with breaking with his first *dharma* father, with some of the painful and confusing aspects of his training with Kapleau, and the difference between Kapleau's understanding of the *dharma* and the subtleties of teaching, and his own. Kapleau had a very passionate but also a militaristic style of teaching, and people would be beaten black and blue with the Zen stick during *sesshins*. Henry came to realize that Kapleau began to teach before his own Zen training was complete. While Kapleau had had a very powerful awakening, there was something incomplete in his understanding of the *dharma* and of teaching.

In Zen, *kensho* and *satori* are by no means the end of the road. Henry suggested that he and many others were casualties of this incomplete training on Kapleau's part. BUT, what was more interesting and helpful was Henry's example of clear-eyed love, respect, and gratitude for Kapleau, even while knowing of his limitations. (Which it would seem were far less serious than Andrew's; my point here is not to compare Kapleau with Andrew, but to share Henry's approach.) Henry had dealt with most of this before Kapleau's death, but there was still a bit further for him to go in coming to total peace with his *dharma* father.

So, during this *sesshin* where I was doing the work I needed to do about my relationship with Andrew, Henry was finishing the work he needed to do around Kapleau. In the mornings we listened to Kapleau's *dharma* talks, and in the evenings Henry would comment on them and put them in the context of his own teaching and that of Robert Aitken. He really modeled a way of being around this that avoided nothing, and was at the same time incredibly compassionate for both himself and Kapleau, wise, mature, respectful, grateful. So this going on in the *sesshin* was like a container for me to go through my own process. Interestingly, I said very little to Danan Henry Roshi about it in *dokusan* (formal interviews with the teacher). Things just came up and burned off. Toward the end of the *sesshin*, Henry said of Kapleau, with enormous emotion, that he loved him and he owed him. And that Kapleau was fully himself, limitations and all, a great lion of the *dharma*, and could not have been other than he was.

At that moment that was exactly how I felt about Andrew. So, that *sesshin* was very powerful for me. The last couple of days of the *sesshin* were different. I went beyond my attachment to and interest in thought and insight, and glimpsed beyond a deep ego-entrenched fear/shame of my "self" being somehow antithetical to the Absolute. I was able to get past, at least briefly, some blocks that had always hung me up in all my practice with Andrew. I can't say this big opening lasted very long, but I feel the *sesshin* planted my feet firmly on the path again. I regained the path, and my faith, and my willingness to risk again. And now it wasn't attached to a particular person, but just to my own aspiration. I'm doing the Zen training here, gradually. It's so different from Andrew's community. Much more spacious, much more respectful of the individual, definitely not authoritarian. I'm finding my way with having a completely different, non-guru-like relationship with my spiritual guide.

May we all learn how to turn our challenges and travails on the spiritual path, and the path of life in general, into pearls of wisdom and compassion.[46]

---

46 whatenlightenment.net, posted February 2, 2005

10

LEAVING THE GURU
Richard Pitt

I NVITING a spiritual teacher into one's life is a profound and life-altering event, often the culmination of a lifetime of spiritual yearning. Love, joy, surrender and bliss — powerful emotions accompany the recognition of another person as one's spiritual guide. The great Indian sage Ramana Maharshi described the role of the spiritual teacher/guru thus: "So much lies in your power, the rest must be left entirely to the Guru, who is the ocean of Grace and Mercy seated in the heart, as the seeker's own self."[47]

A true spiritual master/guru is able to be that reflection of the seeker's deepest yearnings. But many spiritual teachers have not attained that level of wisdom and so, ultimately, are unable to fulfill the yearnings of the student. Thus, in many (if not most) instances of the teacher/disciple relationship, the disciple at some point experiences disappointment. Also, in some situations, the teacher exploits his/her position of authority due to unresolved psychological issues, which are projected onto the students or the community surrounding the teacher — turning these into magnified extensions of the teacher's issues and causing disillusionment, damage, or both. In such situations, leaving the teacher becomes the only option, but even then the decision to leave can be extremely complex and difficult.

Leaving the teacher can also mean leaving a community of fellow students who have become one's friends and family. This is a very painful separation to make, and it requires courage and steadfastness in the face of resistance and even condemnation from one's teacher and fellow students. And it is also a daunting prospect to the extent that, for many who consider leaving, the

---

47 Guru Ramana and Cohen, S.S., *Sri Ramanasramam*, Tiruvannamalai, 2006

outside world appears to be a void. The student may feel that there is little to go back to in the world beyond the spiritual community, in which camaraderie, shared commitment and intimacy have given one a feeling of "belonging." But once a student has arrived at the conclusion that living in the community is for whatever reason undesirable, staying on is usually not possible for very long.

From my own experience of leaving my spiritual teacher, Andrew Cohen, and from the experiences of others who have also left their teachers, I have observed that for most people there are four discernible stages of *fully* leaving a spiritual teacher, and that this process in its entirety can take years. Ultimately, however, one discovers the decision to leave a teacher to be as powerful a turning point as was the decision to follow one.

STAGE 1: "I AM NOT WORTHY"

Many who leave a spiritual teacher are consumed by feelings of unworthiness. "I am not worthy," the student tells himself. "If I were up to it, I would not have left." The message of some spiritual traditions is that once one has opened oneself to spiritual truths and to a true spiritual teacher, one *cannot* leave. To do so means turning one's back on Truth itself; in other words, there is no viable return from the spiritual path. But what if one is not on the *right* spiritual path? What if the teacher turns out not to be so pure as one originally supposed? Just as humans evolve, so does the spiritual impulse. In such cases, remaining in situations that no longer feel wholesome or fulfilling can cause the student harm.

The limbo of feeling unworthy can last for months or years. The former student might attribute the decision to leave to his own weakness while continuing to regard the teacher as beyond reproach. Meanwhile, adjusting to and identifying with the world beyond the spiritual community is difficult. Perhaps the former student feels superior to it, perceiving it to be mundane and empty, while at the same time feeling inferior relative to his former community's high spiritual ideals. Simultaneously, one may also feel powerless — little money, few or no friends, no job. This can be disorienting and emotionally distressing. Painful though it is, however, enduring this first stage is essential to the process of transitioning out of the spiritual community and into a new existence.

Some who leave return for periods, trying to reconcile conflicting feelings about the teacher, the fellow students or the community's prescribed spiritual practices. They may be reluctant to fully re-immerse themselves in the community or to have contact with the teacher, but they don't want to separate themselves totally either. In still other instances, the teacher continues to exert control over the student and confines the student to a kind of purgatory — neither freedom from the situation nor full participation in community life. This tends to occur when the teacher fears that the student will grow critical of him once beyond his sphere of influence, or in the cases of those who simply can't bring themselves to leave for whatever reason.

There are also those who choose to leave, who don't feel unworthy, and who continue to hold the teacher in high esteem; they have simply moved on. This usually happens in the cases of those not so deeply involved, or who have managed to rationalize their decision to leave while continuing to revere the teacher. There are real contradictions inherent in the endeavor of maintaining this position, but some people seem to be able to do it.

STAGE 2: THE RISING OF SUPPRESSED EMOTIONS

As with the stages of grief, so with the stages of leaving: Anger follows sadness. Time passes. Hindsight reveals truths that one could not or did not want to acknowledge at the time. The former student may find that emotions long suppressed arise in a seething mass. If abuse, exploitation or moral compromise was a part of one's experience inside the spiritual community, the anger may be intense, and it may persist for some time. It is important to the process of seeking liberation from one's teacher to let this anger run its course. While some people pass quickly through this stage, others linger there for a while; it is an individual matter. That said, it has been my experience that anger or similar emotions are important to an honest appraisal of one's experience inside a spiritual community if leaving it came about as a result of disillusionment.

Spiritual authoritarianism by definition creates a black and white, "with me or against me" dynamic. One either embraces the teacher, the teachings and the practices, or one does not. There is no dipping the toe in; there is only total immersion. The same is true of leaving: One has to be willing metaphorically to cut the cord from the guru in order to be free from him. It is usually not enough to claim, simply, that "it wasn't for me." One must also accept the fact of one's prior delusion and deconstruct the causes of one's disappointment. This includes acknowledging that the guru is flawed and that one's belief in his self-professed perfection was misplaced. Otherwise, the guru will maintain at least some aura of authority in the mind of the follower, and true independence will not be possible.

It was only after leaving Andrew Cohen's community that I appreciated the arrogance and delusion that lay at the core of our collective spiritual work. It was only with hindsight that I felt embarrassment at having so blindly adored Andrew, who my fellow students and I believed to be a perfectly realized, fully enlightened being. And it was only after regaining objectivity that I could see the extent of the conformity and lack of autonomy that characterized our community's culture. It was also with the perspective of remove that I was able to appreciate anew the camaraderie, intimacy and sincerity of intention of most of my fellow students.

I liked the majority of people involved in Andrew's community. Distinguishing between the letdown I felt about Andrew — his true nature and his teachings — and the fondness I continued to feel for his students helped me to better cope with my anger. I found that I could be angry with Andrew without negating the whole of my community experience, the relationships I forged during it, and the good that came out of it. Once out of Andrew's community, rather than isolating myself from others who had left and who were carrying the weight of similar experiences, I sought their help and their insights. Doing so helped me immeasurably to process my emotions and understand my experiences.

It is important to pay heed to one's anger, and equally important thereafter to let it go. Being the pissed-off apostate not only gets boring, it gives the guru back his power. As one works with one's anger, the goal must be forgiveness of the guru and of oneself. The latter means taking responsibility for the decision to follow the guru while also appreciating the fact that the experience, however flawed, was nevertheless an important part of one's personal evolution. Forgiving oneself and the guru also means refusing to be a victim.

STAGE 3: REINTEGRATION

With the third stage comes reintegration into society at large. The "real world" beckons, and with it, the exigencies of earning a living, establishing meaningful relationships, finding sexual intimacy, and so on. Some make this transition with ease, but for the majority of people whose commitment to the spiritual community was deep and total, this is a more difficult crossing to make. Generally, successful reintegration can only come after the hard work of the first two stages has been accomplished.

Spiritual arrogance and narcissistic self-involvement are common side effects of the "spiritual search." Coming back down to earth, returning to the everyday world after a long period away from it, helps the former student to reconcile two aspects of life: the spiritual and the worldly.

During this third phase, questions remain about the feasibility of the guru/disciple relationship in general. For some, the very thought of following another teacher induces nausea. One profoundly difficult experience with a guru closes some seekers to the possibility of ever undertaking such a journey again. Others, however, embark on a search for another teacher guided by the lessons learned from the previous experience. Those who do must still be vigilant for signs that the new teacher is motivated by ego and narcissism. Some have found that opening themselves to another spiritual teacher has allowed them to forgive their previous one. A new teacher can help foster healing in the student. Therapy may be also useful in helping a person move on. For others, healing can come from devotion to a meaningful cause.

In other words, the search for meaning in one's life continues. Spiritual yearning doesn't go away just because one has left a spiritual community. Redirecting one's spiritual path, discovering a new spiritual focus, redefining one's direction and purpose—all of these are crucial elements of the third stage.

STAGE 4: ACHIEVING OBJECTIVITY

One has arrived at the fourth stage when it is possible to survey one's experiences with objectivity and to do so without resentment, anger, judgment or other negative emotions. During this fourth stage, one sees the larger puzzle of one's life and is able to put that piece of it—time with the guru, time away from the world at large—into its proper context. Instead of being defined by the experience, one recognizes the spiritual journey as part of the complexity and diversity of one's life. At this stage, relationships with fellow former students can exist without being defined by the past. To acknowledge one's anger over abuses and hypocrisy no longer entails being embittered by that knowledge or feeling oneself to be a victim of it. While this does not preclude the desire to expose the truth or to shed light on other spiritual authorities that abuse their positions, doing so is not an all-consuming need in one's life. One is free.

Freedom means that one's spiritual life endures, unfettered by the chains of anger, sorrow and resentment over previous experiences. One may choose to embark on a new journey or to embrace another spiritual teacher. One may revise one's notion of spiritual life, including concepts of enlightenment and the presumption that "the enlightened state" as one previously conceived it is attainable. During this stage, anything is possible—and one thing is certain: Having once been with a flawed spiritual teacher, one's eyes are wide open in any search for another, especially when it also means embracing a community that surrounds a teacher. The innocence and naïveté that characterized the initial search are replaced by a knowingness, a clear-headedness. It is also during this stage that one realizes that human perfection as previously conceived may not exist and that, therefore, neither may the perfect teacher. However, it is also important not to be cynical about finding the right spiritual teacher, one who can truly assist in one's spiritual evolution whether perfectly realized or not.

One of the great lessons from my own time with Andrew Cohen was the realization that I do not necessarily require a spiritual authority outside of myself—that life inevitably brings the challenges we need to face. I no longer need to seek the answers beyond myself, in the form of a living teacher; there are many ways to find spiritual inspiration outside of a teacher/disciple relationship.

MOVING THROUGH THE FOUR STAGES

It can take years to complete the four stages of leaving. After a decade of commitment, for example, it can take as many as five years to move through them all completely. The first stage is often the shortest, because most people, having come to the decision to leave, do so quickly. In some instances, however, a student might flirt with the notion of leaving without ever summoning the courage to do so, or taking years to act on one's recognition that leaving is necessary.

The second stage takes longer and depends on the student's community experiences. If the student suffered or witnessed abuses while in the spiritual community, the process of coming to terms with anger and disappointment can be a long one. Because of this, the second stage may run into the third—working through feelings of anger and resentment while also working to reintegrate into society. This third stage can take a number of years and depends on the student's circumstances prior to joining the spiritual community. For some, especially for younger students who might not have had a history of employment or social connections, it can be very difficult to establish roots where none previously existed. Another challenge of reintegration is finding experiences that match the intensity and profundity of those that one had inside the spiritual community. Finding the same levels of significance and inspiration in day-to-day life can be difficult.

Once one has arrived at the fourth stage, one has definitively established a new way of life. Onward!

11

A MISPLACED GRATITUDE

In so many cases, discipleship unknowingly becomes a form of spiritual slavery. Too many are unwilling to question the perfection of the attainment of their teacher for fear of threatening the perceived link with the absolute that the teacher represents.

–Andrew Cohen[48]

THERE are as many spiritual teachers as there are spiritual paths. At one end of the spectrum are teachers who mentor their students and share their knowledge and insight with them without making any demands of "surrender." And at the opposite end is the authoritarian guru who embraces a more confrontational approach, "taking the student on" and laying considerable claim to the individual's autonomy and day-to-day life.

If the path, under the guidance an authoritarian guru, entails sacrificing one's autonomy, one might well ask: Why follow it? On the other hand, thousands the world over have submitted themselves in this way, and in some cultures surrender to a guru is considered the only true spiritual path. If it is presupposed that the seeker is by definition "lost in ego," it seems to follow naturally that he or she cannot be expected to arrive at Self-realization alone—justifying the conclusion that only a profoundly liberated spiritual authority can guide one to enlightenment.

Psychologist Len Oakes proposes an alternative rationale (which, as I have indicated elsewhere in this book, may or may not be applicable across the full spectrum of spiritual paths and practices). According to Oakes's model, the seeker who submits to an authoritarian guru is primarily motivated by the desire to

---

48 Cohen, Andrew, *An Unconditional Relationship to Life: The Odyssey of an American Spiritual Teacher*, Lenox, MA: What Is Enlightenment? Press, 1995, p. 50 (online: "A Crisis of Trust," enlightennext.org/magazine/j9/andrew_crisis.asp)

engage in a "great work," a project that summons the student's inner resources and speaks to his or her most profound concerns about life. The teacher inspires the essential confidence that the student can—indeed, must—do this "great work," but it is the student who cultivates the commitment and integrity required to see it through.

If, in either case, the teacher inspires a desire for transformation in the student, and the student (to whatever degree) realizes this goal, one might ask: Who deserves the credit—the teacher, for spurring the student to action, or the student, for doing the work? As I have learned in conversations with many of Andrew Cohen's former students, the answer depends on the individual. Some have expressed the conviction that, despite having left Cohen's community, they owe Cohen a large debt of gratitude. I contend, on the other hand, that such gratitude is at least partly misplaced: I believe (using Oakes's model) that the gratitude of former students who have achieved some measure of their "great work" is more appropriately directed toward themselves and to those fellow community members who most fostered their progress.

Assessing one's past experience with a guru in terms of one's personal evolution can be a challenging task, and may entail a reassessment of one's basic assumptions regarding the spiritual path. In some cases, for example, it may prove necessary to examine anew one's faith in the notion that such a person as a "perfectly enlightened teacher" actually exists. Though there is, again, a spectrum of views on this subject, in most cases it is not difficult to discern a teacher's flaws. While some teachers forthrightly acknowledge their shortcomings, others, such as Andrew Cohen, not only deny the possibility of their own fallibility, but advance tacit or explicit claims to flawlessness. In his book *An Unconditional Relationship to Life*, Cohen implies that he has attained a condition that "perfectly reflects the Absolute."[49] Similarly, in his "Declaration of Integrity"—a rebuttal to former students' charges of his responsibility for abuses inside his community—he implies

---

49 Cohen, *ibid..*, p. 140

that he possesses unblemished integrity, putting the onus on the observer to decide whether his conduct actually lives up to his insinuations or outright claims of perfection.[50] In this book, I make the case that the answer to this question is no.

What does this imply for the student? How does the awareness of a guru's limitations and contradictions affect one's perception of his or her experiences with the guru? In my own case, I am reminded of the Buddha's famous enjoinder to "be a light unto *yourself.*" Those of us who lived in Andrew Cohen's community for a number of years no doubt had experiences that were catalyzed by his power and presence. I believe, however — knowing what we now know about Andrew — that our gratitude for such experiences is due primarily to the community of friends with whom we shared them, rather than to him. What seemed to be an electric current of spiritual power emanating from Andrew and his confidence was not, after all, based on goodness or integrity. As Oakes puts it in *Prophetic Charisma,* "[T]he leader is not a great man; he is a great actor playing the role of a great man."[51] In the final analysis, such seems to be the case with Andrew Cohen.

What, then, was the spark that ignited our individual and collective spiritual fire? If not Andrew Cohen's flawless nature — if not, as he would have it, his "perfect reflection of the Absolute" — then what? I conclude that it must have come from *our* goodness, from the open hearts of his disciples, and from our idealism. I do not say this out of vanity. We wanted very much for Andrew Cohen to be the man and the spiritual leader that he claimed to be, and we gave him wide margins for error because his failure to live up to his claims of perfection would be, in essence, our failure, too: If he was not the perfectly enlightened guru that he insisted he was, then why had we given up so much in our lives to follow him? Andrew Cohen has never strayed from his message that all that happened around him was, in effect, because of him. Ultimately, however, it does not seem possible to attribute the power and profundity of our experiences to "the guru's

---

50 "A Declaration of Integrity," andrewcohen.org/blog, posted October 18, 2006
51 Oakes, *op. cit.,* p. 37

grace," because the corrosive effect of Andrew's flaws ultimately ate away at whatever "grace" might have existed. Andrew Cohen *did not* emanate perfection, nor is he the manifestation of an idealized evolutionary potential. That is the painful realization that only time has enabled me to grasp.

What is also true, and what must be stated in fairness to Andrew and to those who continue to believe in him, is that he did play a *part* in the transformation that took place among us, and in the love and communion that were shared. But it is important, I feel, not to go too far in granting him credit. After all, he continues to defend his most dubious conduct, and he continues to deny allegations of abuse. Thus, for many of his former students, gratitude is mixed with confusion, and with a nagging reminder of Andrew's lies, excesses and misguided teaching methods. We are the "shadow *sangha*," as he calls us, and his disparagement of us further dilutes what gratitude we might permit ourselves to feel and that he might deserve.

Andrew's reasoning goes like this: Those who criticize me are spiritual failures who cannot stand to see their own egos exposed. What rather seems to be the case, however, is that Andrew cannot bear to be seen as anything less than perfect. That is his pathology. It drives the guru/disciple dynamic within his community, it accounts for his vehement denials of abuse, and it underlies his fear of being exposed. I would argue that Andrew's notion of a "shadow *sangha*," and of what he calls the spiritual "failure" of his former students, is actually a projection: He fears his own failure and is in denial of his own shadow — a community of ex-followers who were once devoted to him and are now estranged from him, living full lives without him as their center, free from his gravitational pull.

In *The Castle in the Forest*, Norman Mailer writes, "A mediocre mind, once devoted entirely to one mystical idea, can obtain a mental confidence well beyond its normal potential."[52] This is the dynamic at play in Andrew Cohen's community, where authori-

---

52 Mailer, Norman, *The Castle in the Forest*, New York: Random House, 2007

tarianism and an oversimplification of spiritual ideals transfer the individual autonomy of others into his hands. Unfortunately, it is difficult to see this when one is inside his community. All authoritarian ideologies represent themselves as revolutionary marches into history, and their success thus depends on the acquiescence of their followers. The individuals involved lose their moral bearings and discover that they are capable of doing things they would not otherwise have done. It is exhilarating to feel "chosen" — and horrifying to realize in retrospect how blindly and misguidedly one followed.

Despite his claims to the contrary, Andrew Cohen is not invincible. No one is. That being the case, he compensates with grandiosity. He ignores his critics and refers to them as "spiritual failures." When his mother wrote a book that was critical of him, his rebuttal was a book of his own, *In Defense of the Guru Principle*,[53] in which he asserts the indispensability of the guru for human spiritual progress. As Oakes writes,

> The prophet's credibility founders most over his failure to be truly human, that is, to reflect on his behavior, to doubt himself, to concede error, and to show genuine regret for hurt to others. This lack unnerves and embarrasses the followers. They bring with them enormous goodwill and loyalty, but when the leader shows not mere refusal but sheer inability to admit any insufficiency, when vain boasting and ranting, and naïve invincibility alternate with bouts of self-pity and paranoid fantasies, and when the followers' sense that the leader's fantasies are more important to him than their welfare, their affections change...even the most loyal soon begin to question. To continue working for him then becomes a conspiracy to protect him from facing his own delusions. The leader defends his brittle strengths in an increasingly grotesque and inflexible way; the nearer he comes to the core of his pathology, the more catastrophic and extreme his reactions become.[54]

---

53 Cohen, Andrew, *In Defense of the Guru Principle*, Lenox, MA: What Is Enlightenment? Press, 1999
54 Oakes, *op. cit.*, pp. 180-181

It is painful to come to terms with one's experiences with a powerful but imperfect spiritual leader. I left Foxhollow in a state of uncertainty over what had occurred there and who I was as a result of it. What I knew for certain, though, and what sustains me to this day, is that something beautiful can happen when open-hearted, trusting individuals come together to give themselves to a higher purpose. That those of us who devoted ourselves to Andrew Cohen were disappointed by him need not—and does not—diminish the power of our intention.

This book is not an invitation to cynicism. This story—the hard truth of it—deserves to be aired, but it should not be embraced as substantiation of the cynic's claim that spiritual enlightenment or an authentic spiritual approach to living cannot be achieved, or that spiritual communities cannot thrive. They can—just not under the kind of authoritarian conditions described in these pages.

My hope is that this book will inspire conversations about how spiritual communities founded in goodness can find their place in this world. There are so many fine teachers who have integrity and their students' best interests at heart. The path is open to all seekers. Authoritarians are not required to shepherd the seeker to spiritual awakening. My great discovery since leaving Andrew Cohen's community is that the path is wide open—and always has been.

12

THE MOTHER OF GOD
An interview with Luna Tarlo

W HEN I met Andrew Cohen in 1988, one striking older
student stood out: his mother, Luna Tarlo. That she
was his student always intrigued me. I wondered
how it could work. It turns out, it couldn't. Eventually, things
broke down completely and Luna left Andrew's community. A
few years later, she wrote a book about her experiences. When
The Mother of God[55] was published in 1997, it made a small but no-
ticeable splash and was mentioned and reviewed in several publications, including *Psychology Today*. What follows are excerpted
passages of Jill Neimark's article from that magazine's March/
April 1998 issue about the guru/disciple relationship in general,
and Luna Tarlo's relationship with her son in particular:

> ...Luna wryly calls herself the Mother of God (and has written a book
> by that name) because her son, Andrew Cohen, is an American guru
> with an international following, and for three and a half years she
> became his disciple. Today they are estranged and she believes they
> will never speak again. "I've been burned," she says. "I don't believe
> in the premise anymore that anybody can save you. And my son has
> become a monster to me."

> ...In 1986...[Andrew] was just another spiritual seeker who had bro-
> ken up with his girlfriend when he met an Indian teacher named
> Poonja. Later that month he claimed that a "spiritual realization [had]
> transformed his life beyond recognition." He immediately began to
> attract followers, and brought his mother to India, where, she says,
> he told her that the son she knew was dead, that he felt like God,
> and that in his presence she was now enlightened. "At first, I felt I'd
> won some kind of cosmic lottery," recalls Tarlo, who was astonished
> by her son's new charisma and "silver tongue," and who was longing
> to be catapulted out of her own pain (she'd lost her husband, father,

---

55 Tarlo, Luna, *The Mother of God*, New York: Plover/Autonomedia, 1997

and mother in the previous four years and had just left a second marriage). "Andrew said he felt he was on fire, that his body was like an electric generator. Poonja told me he'd been waiting for Andrew all his life." Andrew and Poonja wrote each other ardent letters. From Poonja, November 2, 1986: "You've occupied my whole mind day and night." From Andrew, April 13, 1988: "Master, I love you so! My each breath is only you and you and you!"[56]

By 1989, Luna was sending similar adoring letters to her son: "Beloved: just as a leaf turns toward the sun, am I turned towards you." Surrendering to a spiritual teacher is, she says, as mysterious and shattering an act as falling in love. "Men and women fall in love with Andrew in this mad, hysterical way, as if he's their savior. I did, too. I believed he had reached this exalted state."

...Eventually, Tarlo broke with her guru and son. "I've lost a child and I'll never get over it." But, looking back, she believes she knows why she followed him and why he is still so popular: "Everybody wants to be saved from their suffering, and the unique quality gurus have is that they seem so certain, so confident. Confidence is its own kind of magic."

Luna Tarlo's book made Andrew furious. He called a meeting of his students to refute his mother's claims. Loyal followers, we supported him. It was not until many years later that I read the book, a mother's lament at having lost her son to an absolutist and authoritarian belief system that left no room for familial relationships.

In May 2008, Israeli journalist Yonatan Levy asked Andrew Cohen about his mother's book. An EnlightenNext spokesperson responded on Andrew's behalf that his mother had admitted to having "fictionalized aspects of her book for dramatic effect." In a conversation in the spring of 2009, I asked Luna Tarlo to respond to this and other claims that Andrew had made about her and her book, including his denial of her claim that he had said, "Anyone who loves me is promised enlightenment."

---

56 From Cohen, Andrew, *My Master Is Myself: The Birth of a Spiritual Teacher* (second edition), Lenox, MA: What Is Enlightenment? Press, 1995

William Yenner: *How do you respond to the claim that you admitted to fictionalizing aspects of your book for dramatic effect?*

Luna Tarlo: This book is something I couldn't have made up. If it ever comes to it, I will go to court with my notebooks to defend the accuracy of what I wrote. I have kept all the notebooks. I recorded something about what transpired every day. I'd never kept a diary before, but for some reason during that time I did.

WY: *Andrew has denied saying certain things that you attribute to him in your book. Let's consider specific remarks he denies having made, starting with, "Meeting Poonja made up for a lifetime of not being recognized."*

LT: Again, I could never have made that up. There must have been a great sense of him having been somehow ignored, or rather his potential ignored. He'd never said anything like that to me before. It was pretty extreme, but I do think he suffered, for some reason, from some kind of inferiority complex. Compared to his brother Josh, he didn't function very well in school. I sent him to a progressive private school. And he had a hard time. We—his father and I—were very concerned. We sent him to a child therapist for help, which he ridiculed in front of his followers when I was with him. He made it sound as though I had somehow sinned against him for doing that. Poonja told Andrew he had been waiting for him all his life. I know for a fact that Poonja said the same thing to a number of people who came to visit him. Poonja was pretty unknown at the time; Andrew put him on the map.

WY: *What about, "Anyone who loves me is guaranteed enlightenment"?*

LT: He absolutely said that to me; now he denies it. I couldn't have made that up either. The outrageous audacity appalled me—but I have to confess, in spite of that, that I was strangely stirred. That was at the very beginning.

WY: *"You know, Luna, sometimes I feel like a god."*

LT: All of this was at the beginning. He wanted his mother to know these things.

WY: *"Tonight during* satsang *my personal desires died."*

LT: Can you imagine? He said those words! More grandiosity.

WY: *You said, "I'm happy because I trust you," and he replied, "That's the only reason you're happy."*

LT: I was coming unglued at this point. I thought, well, maybe what he was saying was true, and I was frightened.

WY: *"Either you give way to me or our relationship cannot continue."*

LT: When he said this I felt dangerously threatened. For a long time I couldn't deal with it. I was being forced to surrender. Deep down I wasn't convinced. No matter how low I bowed before him, I was never totally convinced, and he could feel it.

WY: *What are your memories of the time in India before Andrew met Poonja?*

LT: I once said to Andrew, before he met Poonja, "When you go to India, I would love to come and visit for a few weeks, if it's okay with you." I was being careful, not wanting to force the issue. At the end of a year, he told me to come, and it was on this trip to India that I met Alka, who was to become Andrew's wife some years later. When I arrived it seemed to me, within a day or two, that this woman hated me. Andrew admitted later that she suffered from extreme jealousy, but as if it were just a bad habit. However, once he even used the word, paranoid. But she regarded me as an enemy from the beginning. She knew that Andrew really loved me. I was very shocked at everything that happened after that.

WY: *What happened?*

LT: This was a turning point. He suddenly got very hard, very aggressive, forcing me to go to Christopher Titmus's retreat in Bodh Gaya. He gave me no choice. I felt intimidated by him for the first time in my life, very uneasy at the change in our relationship. This retreat was for four out of the six weeks I was to be in India. He wanted me to spend a month with Christopher Titmus, a narcissistic meditation teacher I disliked. But Andrew admired Christopher enormously. He wanted to be like him; Titmus was his ideal. Of course, this was before he met Poonja. What is interesting here is that this characteristic of being so insistent, completely regardless of my wishes, seemed a sudden aberration on his part. After all I had been invited to see India with him and I got the impression that he wanted to show me why he loved it. By the end of the retreat Andrew and Titmus were enemies, and Andrew and Alka were estranged. There was an incident when the two of them — Andrew and Christopher — had a fight and were actually, fists raised, going to hit each other.

WY: *Was this the trip when you first met Andrew's friend Murray Feldman, who had already met Poonja? And was this when Murray first told Andrew about Poonja?*

LT: Yes. Andrew, Alka and I had gone to spend a couple of days in Ramana Maharshi's ashram before going to the retreat. That's when we met Murray. I think Andrew had met him before or had heard about him from someone. The conversation they had was private, but Andrew told us a little about it. Murray had raved to him about a fantastic guru he called "Poonjaji."

WY: *Andrew looked up to Murray at that point?*

LT: Oh, yes, very much. Later on, after Murray had become Andrew's disciple, I remember saying to Andrew that Murray was going to be his "John the Baptist." It seemed like that at the time.[57] This was not long after Andrew's "transformation." I'd gone back home after Christopher Titmus's retreat, leaving Andrew pretty miserable about Alka and not knowing what to do next. About three months later, Andrew wrote, telling me to come back. He had already sent me several twenty-page letters describing what

---

57 Murray Feldman left Andrew Cohen's community less than three years later; he subsequently returned to Poonja and remained his student until Poonja's death in 1997.

had happened to him. "You have to come right back now!" he said during a phone call. I went right back. And that's when I had the shock of seeing a colossal change in him. I noticed it right away. I remember being astounded when some people who had taken some rooms with him on the roof of a temple came and greeted him with the most extreme deference. During the three months we had been apart, my son seemed to have been elevated in the eyes of others to the stature of a man of great wisdom, a holy man. People bowed to him; I didn't know what to make of it. It seemed some kind of miracle. He had all at once lost every semblance of his former insecurity. He spoke in a tone of absolute certainty. His confidence overwhelmed me. He no longer "felt" like my son. It seemed good, at first, to see people looking up to him, honoring him—it was like something you see in the movies.

WY: *In* The Mother of God, *you write that Andrew demanded complete surrender from you. You made some very big concessions to him—you intended to get rid of your apartment in New York, you submitted to his public berating of you, and you threw out all of your unpublished writings. In the book, you write, "From the filing cabinet to the incinerator, it took five trips to annihilate a total life's work."*

LT: That was the worst thing I ever did in my life. But I couldn't *not* do it; it represented my independence and Andrew wanted me to destroy my work as an act of surrender to him. It was completely self-destructive, but there could be no other legitimate love than the love for Andrew in his cult. It really was horrible. I burned everything. Three novels. The enormity of it shocks me even now. It was the worst thing I ever did to myself. I remember the mood I was in, a trance of horror. I felt that he had me by the neck and I was choking to death. But a real miracle happened. I found out years later that I had given my daughter-in-law copies of the novels. I had completely forgotten about it; so had she. One day I went to a party my daughter-in-law (my other son's wife) gave, and she informed me that she had found a cardboard box with some of my work in it. The three novels were inside intact. I think I screamed with joy. To this day I still have no memory of ever giving them to her—nor does she—but that makes it all the more miraculous. I recovered everything.

WY: *What about the apartment?*

LT: My other son, hearing that I was going to give up my New York apartment, kept paying the rent. He and his wife had the feeling, they said later, that I would need it again someday. Otherwise, I wouldn't have it now. It's a beautiful apartment and it doesn't cost much money.

WY: *How and when did you decide to leave Andrew?*

LT: I was in California with my new housemates when I heard about the teacher U.G. Krishnamurti. I was collecting many grievances, but I wasn't ready yet to say no to Andrew. It was very difficult for me. I knew if I said no it would be the end of our relationship. I knew I'd never see him again. For me to separate from him was huge.

WY: *Did Andrew know he was losing you?*

LT: I think he guessed from the way I expressed myself, by the way I was attracted to things outside the immediate world he presented us with. I went to the gym. I did things that were just fun. Everything that one does that is not connected to him is "evil."

WY: *You write in your book that "Andrew turned the ordinary not only upside down, but into something villainous."*

LT: What I mean is that little ordinary pleasures like tap-dancing lessons, or playing the piano or seeing old friends, somehow, in Andrew's eyes became evil distractions that took us away from him. That's the essential thing that was going on all the time. He wanted us to concentrate only and singularly on HIM. One of the reasons I didn't suffer after I left was that I'd had to deal with all of that beforehand. I had to accept that I could not accept Andrew as my teacher, dominating my every move, constantly humiliating me in public, etc. And I couldn't bear to watch him doing the same things to others. That meant I had to give him up. And I knew it would be forever. Still, I couldn't just leave, just like that. It wasn't easy. Before I could take such a drastic step I had to be totally clear emotionally about why I was leaving and face ahead of time what the consequences would be. After I left I never looked back. I knew I had done the only thing that had to be done. I knew there was no other choice. I never doubted myself afterwards. I had worked it all out. The final stimulus was meeting U.G. Krishnamurti about a week after my arrival in California. Once it happened, once I met U.G., my infatuation with Andrew and his cult was over. I have this memory of four of my housemates and myself going to visit U.G. and afterwards standing outside his little house struck by what we had heard. Suddenly, almost simultaneously without a word spoken, we all realized we had decided to leave Andrew. We didn't talk about it. We all stood, looking at each other. It was an amazing moment. I'd had a lot of respect for U.G.; I'd read his books, and I knew he was an amazing man. I can't say, "When I met U.G., I saw the light." No, it wasn't like that; but I knew my life with Andrew was over.

WY: *How did you feel after leaving Andrew?*

LT: I was the only one of the five of us who didn't suffer from some feeling of regret or confusion afterwards. Every time Andrew had done something I considered shameful, I'd have to stuff it away somewhere inside myself. Lots of things happened that bothered me, particularly the use of physical abuse as a way of breaking the ego. For example — this happened after I left — asking the women to go into a freezing lake in late October and stand waist deep, and submerge themselves completely again and again for an entire hour — that is an exercise in torture.[58] The way he treated people I thought was horrible. And what about using humiliation to break someone — to take away somebody's dignity? It's a horrible thing to do to a person. That's what he did over and over again, not just to me, but to everybody. And I didn't even know then how far he was going with other people.

---

58 See *Chapter 3.*

WY: *How did Andrew respond to your leaving?*

LT: When I left, I told him I didn't need a teacher any more, and he said, "Wait 'til you crash!" How could I make stuff like this up? You can see how much violence my leaving brought up in him.

WY: *Are you angry?*

LT: I'm no longer angry, and that means I've forgiven him. You can't live with that anger. In time I saw that it might have been inevitable for him to go the way he went—who knows? People are mysterious and unpredictable. So the anger left me. I want him to stop hurting people, and to me that is very important. And it's important for this to get publicized.

WY: *When did you last see Andrew?*

LT: I last saw him in about 1998 when we met for a dinner in New York. At the dinner, we could not talk about anything. Everything was too loaded. The only thing we agreed on was a movie. As I walked home after dinner I realized how heartbreaking it was to know I would probably never see him again, but I knew it was the truth.

WY: *How do you think Andrew feels about you now?*

LT: I know this is a terrible thing to say, but I think he's waiting for me to die. As a matter of fact, you can use that as my final comment. He's going to be very happy if I die, and he's probably waiting for it. Why? Because I'm the bone in his throat, the thorn in his side. I'm his mother; he loved me very much, and I loved him in the same way, but I'm sure he regards my leaving as a betrayal. That's the way he thinks—he thinks that I betrayed him. What does he do with this? He tells people his mother is crazy and leaves it at that. Still, I imagine that when he goes to bed at night he gives me a thought now and then. It's as hard to forget a mother as it is for a mother to forget a son.

WY: *What do you see as Andrew's legacy, and how do you view him now?*

LT: As far as I'm concerned, he's responsible for destroying people. I have no feeling about him anymore; he's just a very bad person. His presence on this earth isn't good for anyone. He can't afford to face what he has become. What can he do? He is in up to his neck. It's very dangerous to let in a little crack of light; then the whole house of cards falls apart. People still think he's charming. I don't.

WY: *Final thoughts?*

LT: I'm not angry anymore. It's just that this man is damaging people. It's the old story of power corrupts, etc. I don't know how it all happened, but I hold Poonja responsible — to what extent, I don't know. Andrew naïvely swallowed up everything Poonja said to him. I guess it was what he wanted to hear. But Poonja was playing with fire. One day I'm afraid Andrew is going to go too far and get into a lot of trouble.

13

LIFE AFTER ANDREW

L EAVING the EnlightenNext cult has been one of the most powerful and positive experiences of my life. Looking back on my first days after leaving Foxhollow, I see that I was at a crossroads. My life was in total flux. I had rejected the authoritarian system of my guru, and I faced the wide-open prospect of the rest of my life, whatever it might turn out to be. Though for years I had been warned by Andrew that leaving him would be the mistake of a lifetime, and would mean turning my back on all that is holy and sacred, I hadn't fallen for it. Though I did wonder from time to time whether I'd made the right decision, something inside me said that it had been no mistake, that I'd made the right choice and that true freedom and healing were now in store for me.

The sheer emptiness I felt was actually a balm to my soul, and as the first hours and days passed, I began to experience a sense of boundless freedom and joy. I was the captain of my own ship, and I felt liberated in a way that surprised and amazed me. The relief I felt at having escaped Andrew's grip propelled me into a nearly constant state of bliss for several months. *"Oh my God,"* I thought. *"I am so grateful. I'm back. Life is here, love is here. Once again, I can be who I am."* The recovery of one's autonomy is the sweetest thing!

Initially I traveled, reconnecting with friends and family, all of whom were incredibly welcoming and understanding despite my having ignored them for more than a decade. Their acceptance was a source of healing for me, and it was also a humbling lesson. I had been a really arrogant guy, and I owed many people apologies. I also had my inner work cut out for me: While I was free to be myself, I still had many deeply ingrained Andrew-centric ideas to purge, which it would take time and persistence to dig up and discard. A telling barometer of my residual loyalty to Andrew in spite of all his abuse and ill treatment was my response, some months after leaving, to an old friend who had dared to utter a dig about him: I was so offended and taken aback that I almost took her to task for it. Such vestiges of loyalty took me a long time to undo, and it was only through seeing how conditioned and irrational they were that I began to unravel to its source my profound identification with Andrew and his mission. Though I had left the *ashram* decisively, I still required more time to root out all the remaining emotional entanglements.

Particularly helpful to me during this time of examination were my discussions with friends—both former students and those who had never been students—from which many interesting insights and observations emerged. Those who had never been part of Andrew's world contributed a fresh view free from any trappings, providing me with a mirror, while my talks with other former students helped, as they continue to do, with the task of penetrating the residual complexity of our community experiences.

Approximately two years after I'd left, in early 2003, I heard from two fellow former students who, like me, had occupied leadership positions in Andrew's community. Andrew had invited each of them for a sit-down, and both reported that he had spoken negatively of his former students, referring to us as the "shadow *sangha*." He had encouraged both of these former students to withdraw their commitments to attend an upcoming reunion of former students that was being planned in Costa Rica. Since these two were the organizers of the event, he was in effect doing everything he could to get this reunion completely cancelled. It struck me how important it was to him to retain some degree of control over us, and I realized that he found our plan to get together without him extremely threatening. There was something about the combination of his referring to us with contempt as the "shadow *sangha*," and his efforts to halt our evolving relationships, that left me angry and determined not to allow my newfound freedom to falter in the face of his pressure and disparagement. In response, I grew even more determined to set my own course, independent of his controlling influence. This had a powerful effect on me, and I was moved yet again by my growing awareness and recollection of the harsh and bitter treatment that I had endured as Andrew's student.

When I had first left, it had seemed important to let go of resentment and simply to try to move on, but these recent events were more demanding of a response, a declaration of where I actually stood. I was increasingly aware of the inexcusability of Andrew's behavior on many counts. Not only had he mistreated me as his student, he was continuing his efforts to undermine my friends and I, and my growing sense of autonomy now made it possible for me, for the first time, to begin holding Andrew accountable for his actions. This was a new step in my reckoning with what I'd been through, and I dimly sensed its powerful implications for my future. Not only had I left Andrew and embarked on my own life; I was examining what had come before, and relating to Andrew no longer as a disciple but simply as myself. I was no longer using the student/teacher template to determine my approach to our relationship. I felt empowered by my own authority and inner reserves, and I knew that I could confront my former teacher if it came to that.

One thing I'd pondered deeply was the donation of my $80,000 inheritance, which I'd made under conditions of emotional and psychological duress. Upon first leaving, I'd just chalked it up to experience, rationalized that it was probably being used for the common good, and decided internally simply to let go of it. Over time, however, this decision kept resurfacing for further consideration and evaluation. Later in the spring of 2003, as all of my undigested history was boiling up inside me, I decided that I could no longer wait and that I must confront Andrew. The disrespect I knew he'd directed at all of us who'd left was the immediate catalyst, but it had by then become clear to me that a challenge was long overdue. I wrote him a letter in which I expressed my feelings about the abusive treatment I'd been subjected to and my belief that he and his students directed far too much antipathy toward those of us who had left the community. I felt it was outrageous that he would have anything other than kind words for those of us who had given years of our lives to his loyal service, and I declared that in my view his solicitation of my inheritance had been made under duress — which we both knew to be unethical — and demanded its return.

The boldness expressed in my letter was unsettling to me, and I was initially nervous when I sent it, fearing briefly that perhaps Andrew was right after all — I had "turned my back on the holy life," etc. But trusting in myself, I didn't allow this fear to stop me, though I had certainly been rattled by it.

Within a couple of days I received a call from Andrew, offering to return my money as, if I didn't want to donate it, he didn't want to keep it. I was pleasantly surprised to hear this, but he continued in his own defense by asking if I now thought of myself as a victim. To this I replied that I was not a victim, that what I'd written was true, and that I simply wanted my money back. He assured me that I would get it back, and ended the call with a strange and perhaps telling question: Did I want to see him on his knees before the whole world, admitting that he was wrong?

When the paperwork for the return of the donation arrived, however, I saw that there was a string attached: a five-year gag order restricting me from making public statements about Andrew, his teachings or his community. The order seemed to contradict everything that Andrew had ever taught, but I signed the papers and took my donation back.

It was an unprecedented triumph for a former student of Andrew's, and I felt that it represented an important step forward. So many people have endured such harsh treatment and such disrespect and unkindness upon leaving Andrew's community that my successful bid to win back my donation felt like a victory, in some small way, for all of them. But this small victory, such as it was, was only the beginning for me. I still had yet to process most of what had occurred over the course of my thirteen years as Andrew's disciple. I felt as though I were at the base camp of an Everest of unresolved history. As part of my healing process, I wrote an essay about my experiences with Andrew and shared it with a dozen friends, requesting that they keep it confidential. Someone did not, and I received a harsh rebuke from Andrew via his lawyer, whose apparent interpretation of the gag order (not to make public statements) precluded even private communications between friends. I was instructed to desist from disseminating my essay. I was shocked and outraged, but as I didn't want the trouble and expense of a lawsuit, I sent it to no one else.

I feel, in retrospect, that it was beneficial to have been forced to ruminate so quietly for so long. This book is one result of that process. As the years passed, I began writing in greater depth about my experiences (for my own consumption!), and in the spring of 2008, I attended another reunion of former students, this time in Israel. I spent two weeks with around twenty of my friends from Andrew's community, and it was a wonderful, warm and energizing reunion, from which I returned with the conviction that a book about our experiences would be well worth the effort to produce. By the summer of 2008, when my gag order had expired, I was well into writing my contributions to the volume you are holding now.

The thirteen years that I spent with Andrew Cohen remain a part of my life, my mind and my heart. Even with the adversity and the confusion that they brought to my existence, I have benefited from their valuable lessons.

Twenty years ago, a younger man left it all behind to join with a guru in the unfolding of his "holy life." What may look naïve today seemed totally compelling to me then, and I don't believe that I could have done anything differently. From this realization comes compassion for Andrew Cohen and for all of us who participated in his experiment. Even now, I choose not to renounce my years of devotion. How could I? I experienced the freedom of letting go, and I learned a great deal about the deeper meaning of my existence. I would not be the person that I am today without all of it, both the positive and the negative, and regret would rob me of the gratitude that I feel for having been both courageous enough to take that initial leap and wise enough to decide to call it quits. I do, however, feel responsible and sorry for having hurt others in Andrew's community through my complicity in his excesses. And while my story does not end with regret, I hope that the full accounting of it that I've presented in these pages will spare others the prospect of duplicating my mistakes. Time is what we have so little of on this earth; let it not be wasted.

14

QUESTION & ANSWER

Full transcript, Yonatan Levy's "interview" with EnlightenNext

W HAT follows below (*"Exhibit A"*) is a transcript of the responses received by journalist Yonatan Levy to questions he submitted to Andrew Cohen concerning allegations of problematic behavior on Cohen's part in his capacity as a spiritual teacher. Levy submitted his questions in written form after having unsuccessfully sought an interview with Cohen, and received these responses, also in written form, from EnlightenNext's "Communications Director," Amy Edelstein. They were accompanied by a letter from attorney Barry A. Fisher[59] suggesting that Levy's publication of an article on Cohen could result in legal action against his employer, *NRG-Ma'ariv,* an Israeli media site. The text of this letter, dated the same day as Edelstein's answers, is also reproduced below (*"Exhibit B"*).

PDF files of both original documents — EnlightenNext's responses and Fisher's letter — can be viewed and downloaded at the whatenlightenment.net posting of April 22, 2009, "The Truth Will Set You Free," along with background information relevant to the exchange. A PDF file of the contractual gag order referred to in Levy's first question (and said by Edelstein not to exist) can also be found there, linked to the responses of two of Cohen's former students.

Following the publication of these *unaltered original documents,* Tomer Persico, a colleague of Levy's also employed by *NRG-Ma'ariv,* sought a response from EnlightenNext. He received the following intriguing reply: "Everyone has the right to circulate their opinion on the internet. Given the internet medium...the truth and accuracy of information presented differs vastly from site to site for all kinds of reasons." Indeed. Given the role played

---

59 See footnote 13 (*Chapter1*).

by the internet in the propagation of Andrew Cohen's teachings, retreat offerings and fundraising solicitations, EnlightenNext's proviso is an unimpeachable word to the wise: Buyer beware.

It should also be noted that EnlightenNext's statement, "Everyone has the right to circulate their opinion on the internet," apparently doesn't apply to me (William Yenner), whose right to express my "opinion" it successfully sought, by means of a gag order, to repeal for a five-year period; nor to Yonatan Levy, whose proposed article it successfully sought, by means of intimidation, to prevent from being published. The fact that *NRG-Ma'ariv* ultimately declined to post Levy's article comes as a stark reminder that Levy received the "answers" reproduced here from parties who were simultaneously attempting to gag *him*, and who were prepared (as in my case) to use any available option to secure his silence. As long as this condition was presumably satisfied, Cohen and Edelstein felt comfortable telling Levy whatever they cared to — supposedly "in the spirit of cooperation," as their lawyer puts it — without any evident regard for its "truth" or "accuracy."

Since EnlightenNext's attempted gagging of *NRG-Ma'ariv* centered, in all probability, on its expectation that neither its contact with Levy nor the false statements it had given him would ever come to light, it is necessary — especially in this case — to clearly establish whatever common ground there is to be had. At this point, what has been acknowledged by both sides is that these are EnlightenNext's *actual responses* to Levy on Cohen's behalf; this much, one hopes it is safe to say, will never be subject to dispute. Thus, in spite of the fact that "the truth and accuracy of information presented differs vastly from site to site," we finally have two things that everyone can agree on: the authenticity of these documents, and the fact that Andrew Cohen, or someone speaking directly for him, actually issued these statements.

Exhibit A:

June 13, 2008
Questions Submitted to Andrew Cohen or EnlightenNext
Representative by:
Jonathan Yonatan Levy
NRG-Ma'ariv Online News
E: yonatanlevy@gmail.com
W: www.nrg.co.il/online/HP_0.html

Reponses Prepared by:
Amy Edelstein
EnlightenNext Communications Director
T: 1 413 637 6150
C: 1 413 281 0418
E: aedelstein@enlightennext.org
W: www.enlightennext.org

Before responding to each question, EnlightenNext believes that it is important to describe some of the fundamental values that guide this organization and rules that EnlightenNext abides by.

First, the goal of EnlightenNext is the spiritual fulfillment of each individual who joins the organization through the process of Evolutionary Enlightenment. We are unwavering in our commitment to this principle and recognize that there are multiple paths for achieving spiritual fulfillment open to each individual. As such, EnlightenNext has always encouraged its students to be independent and be personally responsible for all their actions, because only through their own increased understanding, self-examination, and meditation can they truly achieve personal enlightenment. On occasion, students have determined that their spiritual development leads them in a different direction. Andrew Cohen respects these individuals' decision and supports them in their spiritual journey. A few disaffected ex-students have initiated campaigns to discredit Andrew Cohen and EnlightenNext. Below sets the record straight.

Second, EnlightenNext has been incorporated as a 501(c)3 or charitable educational organization for many years. We take this tax-exempt status seriously and would never do anything that might jeopardize it. Our books are audited annually by an independent auditing firm, and we rely on outside legal counsel to make certain we are in compliance with the law at all times. For anyone to suggest otherwise belies a complete lack of knowledge of EnlightenNext. We publish an annual report with audited financials which is available through our Development Department. Our filings are always available to the public from the IRS as well as online through Guidestar.org.

Q: *Is it true that students are put under pressure to give large sums of money? What is the ethical justification of it? Is it true that in one case the money was given back under the condition an ex-student would sign a gag order?*

A: No, students are absolutely not put under pressure to give large sums of money. That would go against everything that EnlightenNext and Andrew Cohen stand for. All donations are given freely, and the vast majority of our donations are small. Among the hundreds of donors over the 22 years since the organization was founded, there have been no more than three instances where students have left the organization for their own reasons and demanded to have their donations returned. This is after they participated to the full extent in the intellectual and spiritual life offered by EnlightenNext. No nonprofit like EnlightenNext could survive if donors could be active members over a period of time and then expect to have any donations refunded to them when they choose to move on to other paths. These donations support our daily operations, including our publications, websites, speaking tours, Foxhollow center, and staff of 40 people. We wish those who have left EnlightenNext success in their chosen path to spiritual growth but we have an obligation to the organization and to its current members, staff, and students.

To reiterate our values—our mission and goal is the spiritual evolution of each individual who joins EnlightenNext. EnlightenNext has always encouraged its members to be independent in their understanding and their pursuit of their chosen spiritual path. EnlightenNext values the support and engagement of its members and also recognizes that there are multiple paths for development open to all individuals and as such recognizes that individuals may change their chosen path after some commitment in time.

The third part of the question is absolutely untrue. There has never been a "gag order" or for that matter any other court order issued that was part of any arrangement with any student of EnlightenNext. The question implies that there was some kind of pressure on an individual that resulted in the necessity of some kind of order being issued by judge or jury but that has never been the case.

Q: *Was it common, or is it still common, to give Andrew valuable gifts?*

A: No, it is not and was not common to give Andrew Cohen valuable gifts.

Q: *Is it true that students were in the habit of paying fines of thousands of dollars as correction for things they have done? For example, for leaving Andrew?*

A: No, that is not the case.

Q: *a) Is it true you have described yourself as a unique teacher in regard to the liberation of women? b) Is it true Vimala Thakar criticized your treatment of women, yet this criticism was concealed from the women themselves?*

A: a) Yes.* (*See articles on the Next Women's Liberation published in Folio award-winning magazine What Is Enlightenment by bestselling feminist author Dr. Elizabeth Debold). b) No, it is absolutely not true. Vimala Thakar's correspondence about this issue, which contains many varied nuances including praise for Andrew Cohen's work and insights on women's liberation as well as critiques, was posted in full in a public area for all of Andrew Cohen's students—both women and men—to read.

Q: *Is it true you perceive your spiritual state higher than that of Ramana Maharshi, claimed that "anyone one who loves you is promised enlightenment," and that surrender to you can destroy one's karma?*

A: No. Absolutely not. Andrew Cohen considers Ramana Maharshi a saint of the highest order. He has drawn philosophical distinctions between Vedantic Enlightenment and Evolutionary Enlightenment but those are philosophical distinctions which don't have anything to do with personal spiritual attainment.

Andrew Cohen has never said he has the capacity to destroy anyone's karma. One of the fundamental principles of Evolutionary Enlightenment, and a central tenet of Andrew's teaching, is that each individual must face and take responsibility for the consequences of his or her own actions. (In Eastern traditions, the consequences of one's actions are known as one's "karma.")

Q: *What is Andrew Cohen's present stance concerning "Crazy Wisdom"?*

A: Please clarify what is being referred to by the term "crazy wisdom" to ensure that we have a clear and common definition of the term.

Q: *How is the induction of "healthy shame" useful in enlightening people and freeing them from personal drama?*

A: Traditional religions foster moral development through various teachings that promote conscience or healthy shame. For example, Catholics rely on the practice of Confession, Jews pray for Atonement on the holy day of Yom Kippur, Buddhists, Hindus, and Muslims all have various practices devoted to cultivating a sense of conscience in their adherents. Andrew Cohen firmly believes that developing conscience is an important aspect of spiritual life. Conscience, or healthy shame, as he has on occasion referred to it, is when an individual sees and understands the effects of their negative actions and feels healthy remorse about suffering they have caused to others as a result of their own selfishness, greed, or irresponsibility.

Q: *Does Andrew find himself partially or wholly responsible of the sudden decline of Caroline Franklyn's health, leading to her death?*

A: No, absolutely not. This suggestion flies in the face of the facts. Andrew Cohen was deeply saddened by Caroline Franklyn's death. Caroline Franklyn was a frail older woman who had survived the brutality of the Nazi regime in WWII. Great care was always taken throughout her association with EnlightenNext to accommodate her physical condition while also allowing her to learn from and benefit from its programs. When her health took a sudden decline several of her closest friends from the EnlightenNext center in London traveled over an hour to see her. Her passing was unexpected and was mourned by her friends. Andrew was unaware of her rapidly declining health, as at that time he was elsewhere in the world. Had he heard he certainly would have contacted her as he feels strongly about his obligation as a spiritual guide to support all his students.

Q: *Is Jane O'Neil lying when she says that she was pressured to give a $2,000,000 donation to Andrew? Is she lying when she says that Andrew has violated his promise to her to keep the donation secret?*

A: Ms. O'Neil gave her donation freely of her own accord. To do otherwise would violate the very foundations of EnlightenNext's philosophy and teaching. Ms. O'Neil had been closely involved with EnlightenNext for some years, had graciously contributed at various times, and was involved in its search for a center. Her offer of support was in keeping with her spirit of generosity and EnlightenNext continues to appreciate her gifts. The only persons who knew of the donation were a small group of individuals who were charged with the senior management of EnlightenNext and they neither spread nor published the information. Her donation became common knowledge through her own disclosure to friends, colleagues, family, and eventually on the internet. Ms. O'Neil was a close student for some time and a friend to many at Enlighten-Next. We still have warm feelings towards her and greatly appreciate what her generosity made possible. EnlightenNext wishes her well and hopes she has continued success in her chosen path.

Q: *Is it true that a student who took an oath to refrain from sexual acts but admitted to having masturbated afterwards took out a loan equal to money he was expected to inherit and donated it?*

A: No. Absolutely not.

Q: *Is it true that a student was sent to visit prostitutes daily for 3 weeks against his will?*

A: No, that is absolutely not true.

Q: *Is it true that part of the spiritual practice that Andrew's students did included prostrations before his pictures?*

A: In Hindu, Tibetan, and other Buddhist traditions it is customary to do a spiritual practice of prostrations. It is common in these religions, which have millions of contemporary adherents, to have pictures of one's spiritual mentors in the spiritual practice room. In the early years of EnlightenNext, there were many students who had followed Hindu or Buddhist paths and had done this type of practice before they became part of EnlightenNext. In similar fashion, starting in 1992, for a period of about five years, some students did place photos in their spiritual practice rooms. Andrew himself never advised or recommended using photographs as part of a prostration practice. EnlightenNext has grown and evolved over time, changing its practices to accommodate new members and focus. This particular aspect of practice has not occurred for many years.

Q: *Is it true what Stas (Ernest) Mavrides said, that Andrew revealed to Stas's daughter intimate details about her mother?*

A: No, Andrew never told Stas Ernest Mavrides' daughter information about her mother's intimate life.

Q: *Did Andrew used to determine when his students could engage in sexual relationships, and when they could not?*

A: No, Andrew did not determine for his students. Andrew's students are always encouraged to be independent and responsible in all areas of life. As a spiritual mentor, Andrew would advise his close male and female students in these matters, just as a Rabbi, Priest, Swami, or Buddhist teacher would guide their parishioners in questions regarding marriage or relationship issues.

All spiritual traditions emphasize that sexuality is a fundamental aspect of human life and takes commitment to understand. Andrew has counseled his students to pay attention in this area of life. For example, on one occasion in the late 1990s, Andrew, together with several close male students, each took up a six month period of abstinence to look into the nature of sexual desire. From 1998 to approximately 2001, there was a small group of ten or fifteen close students voluntarily choose to engage more deeply with Evolutionary Enlightenment and to develop their understanding of the sexual drive and the various cultural conditioning surrounding it. Andrew would discuss and advise these particular students more closely on this subject.

An important aspect of the values and principles of EnlightenNext are that sexual relationships between adults are committed and foster respect, peace, and supportive companionship between the partners. There are many married couples at EnlightenNext, and their camaraderie, equality, and partnership is an inspiring example in our postmodern cultural climate. Andrew has published and spoken publicly about the principles that support wholesome relationships of harmony and respect. His teachings on relationship and sexuality can be easily found on at "Happy Endings" and What Is the Relationship Between Sex & Spirituality.

Q: *Were students asked to shave their heads?*

A: Yes, in the early years, around 1992, for a few years, some students shaved their heads as one part of a greater spiritual practice of renunciation, similar to common Buddhist or Hindu spiritual customs. This is no longer the practice and hasn't been for about ten years. Between 1992-1998, some students elected to take vows of celibacy for specific periods of time and as an external sign of this powerful practice of inward renunciation and spiritual commitment--following the tradition of Buddhist and Hindu monks and nuns—these celibate students would shave their heads twice a month. Now some students voluntarily take vows of celibacy for a limited period of time but no longer shave their heads as part of this time-honored practice.

Q: *Was confession of sins a large part of the spiritual practice of Andrew's students?*

A: No, this concept is and was not part of the spiritual practice of Andrew's students.

Q: *Did Andrew ever emphasize the need to absolutely surrender to him?*

A: No. Andrew has always and continues to emphasize individual responsibility for one's own spiritual intention, development, and progress. While individuals can have powerful spiritual openings with teachers, as occurred in Andrew's own case, he has always drawn important distinctions between an inner opening that can serve as a spiritual catalyst and the need for an individual to follow through on their own recognition in order to further their own development. Over the last two decades, Andrew has extensively explored the role of a spiritual teacher or Guru in our post-modern cultural age. As part of his understanding, he has pioneered the notion of what he refers to as the Guru Principle, which he speaks about as being embodied by a collective of individuals who share the same highest aspirations. He has discussed the function of the Guru Principle in detail in public teachings, in his published Guru/Pandit dialogues with evolutionary philosopher Ken Wilber in *What Is Enlightenment?* magazine, and in his book *In Defense of the Guru Principle*.

Q: *Luna Tarlo's book quotes Andrew as saying, "Anyone who loves me is promised enlightenment." As far as you know, did he say these things, and did he say similar things?*

A: No. Andrew never made statements like that promising enlightenment. Luna Tarlo told Andrew that she fictionalized aspects of her book for dramatic effect.

While Andrew never issued any kind of promises like that, it's worthy to note that given his own spiritual path which included association with various spiritual teachers, when he first began teaching in 1986 he would often speak about the profound and illuminating experiences a student can have when they meet a spiritual teacher. At the same time, Andrew always emphasized the importance of individual choice and volition, and the need to act with integrity. He has never and does not now teach that anything can free one from having to take individual responsibility for one's own life and for the effects of one's actions. His focus on this type of spiritual experience shifted significantly soon after he started teaching as he quickly found that students benefit most when they understand the science and mechanics of evolution, the complexity of human development, and become more facile working with a perspective rather than focusing on spiritual experiences themselves.

Q: *Did students used to sit in rooms with cartoons in which they were presented as having sabotaged Andrew, tearing his entrails and throwing his books into the fire?*

A: Andrew has always been an innovative teacher, using all kinds of contemporary cultural expressions to help illuminate to his students ways in which individuals can support or derail their own higher aspirations. One such example, for a few years in the late 1990s, was the use of simple pictures of the postmodern egoic relationship to spiritual life, created by Andrew's long-term students for their personal use. Alongside these pictures were reflections written by these close students describing the enlightened perspective and the unenlightened perspective through their own experience, as well as spiritually inspiring and illuminating quotes from spiritual masters. This area served as a focus of contemplation on the mechanics of the parts of the Self (ego, Authentic Self, and choosing faculty), on cultural and gender conditioning, and on the values of the postmodern age. For many, this served as a powerful teaching tool, providing insight and objective understanding.

Q: *Is it true that there was a circle of men who were required to stand around Andrew's house for two days without moving?*

A: No, the statement that a circle of men were required to stand around Andrew Cohen's house for two days without moving is not true. Students of Andrew Cohen were never required to stand anywhere, without moving, ever. In the summer of 2001, there was a group of male students who did a day and a half spiritual vigil in the grassy yard near Andrew Cohen's house. They were served meals and were free to come and go, and went inside at night to sleep. It is not uncommon for meditators to assume a position of contemplation for a period of time as part of a spiritual practice, discipline, and desire to know.

Q: *As someone who began teaching soon after meeting your teacher, you have never gone through the hardships you require from your students. What makes you sure of their effectiveness?*

A: Andrew was on a committed spiritual path for a decade before he began teaching. Over that time he worked with several teachers and underwent numerous tests and hardships as a student. He freely speaks about his experiences and of what he learned about the spiritual path from it.

Q: *Has the* What Enlightenment??! *blog [whatenlightenment.net] made you more careful or reflective as to your methods or means of teaching?*

A: EnlightenNext has been growing, particularly in the last few years, during which the *What Enlightenment??!* blog was published. We have an email list of 70,000+, and over 10,000 worldwide "evolutionaries," members of our network. And we continue to develop an ever-growing network of friends and colleagues committed to the evolution of consciousness and culture through the publication of Folio award-winning *What Is Enlightenment?* magazine and through our weekly EnlightenNext Webcast with its Honorary Practitioners, distinguished individuals from various fields who serve as educators and advisors.

EnlightenNext and Andrew Cohen are becoming better known, and there is more publicity in many ways. We now have many more students teaching, writing, and speaking in conferences, seminars, and other public events about what the path and practice of Evolutionary Enlightenment is, about our inquiry into the evolution of culture, and what life is like as a committed student of Andrew Cohen. As we grow, and as we have more and more engagement with others who are doing similar work in the culture, we continue to appreciate the perspective from our associates, colleagues, friends, and professional advisors, and the objectivity they generously provide on how best we can accomplish our work and mission. Numerous former students also continue to offer valuable input, advice, and support but the blog referred to is primarily designed by a few disgruntled students who do not support our work and do not wish us to grow in positive ways. We have always had an open door policy to our centers and teachings, and we continue to look for new and better ways to communicate more about this perspective on spiritual and cultural development and the results of our work.

General Links:

enlightennext.org, andrewcohen.org, wie.org

From Andrew Cohen about the Guru Principle and the Development of His Students & EnlightenNext:

• A Declaration of Integrity

• The Guru & Pandit, 20 dialogues with Ken Wilber & Andrew Cohen on the evolution of enlightenment and various emergences and challenges in Andrew Cohen's teaching work

• In Defense of the Guru Principle

• An Unconditional Relationship to Life

From Andrew Cohen's Students:

• A Matter of Integrity, by Carter Phipps

• Boomeritis: More than a Book Review, by Elizabeth Debold

• On The New Women's Liberation, by Elizabeth Debold and others

About EnlightenNext, Evolutionary Enlightenment, and the Growing Movement of "Evolutionaries": Weekly Webcast Discussion, Global Events, Centers

Exhibit B:

FLEISHMAN & FISHER, LAWYERS
1925 CENTURY PARK EAST, SUITE 2000
LOS ANGELES, CALIFORNIA 90067
PHONE (310) 557-1077 FAX (310) 557-0770
Writer's e-mail address: bfisher557@aol.com

June 13, 2008

NRG-Ma'ariv
Galia Azran, Editor
2 Karlibach Street
Tel Aviv, Israel
By e-mail galiaa@nrg.co.il
Yonatan Levy, Writer
NRG-Ma'ariv Online News
2 Karlibach Street
Tel Aviv, Israel
By e-mail yonatanlevy@gmail.com

Re: <u>EnlightenNext and Andrew Cohen</u>

To Jonathan Levy (aka Yonatan Levy) and NRG-Ma'ariv Online News:

This office represents EnlightenNext and Andrew Cohen. You have submitted a series of questions to my clients in connection with a proposed article to be published in NRG-Ma'ariv Online News. These questions are said to arise out of allegations made with respect to my clients by third parties.

We appreciate your diligence and caution in this matter. At any time, but particularly in this age of the internet, innuendo published can cast shadows that overtake public perception, leading to beliefs that are out of alignment with facts or even with the intent of the writer/publisher. Especially in articles that are personality profiles, such as the one proposed, this is even more the case. We are trusting that you will act with prudence and consideration with respect to the facts and reputation of all parties.

In an e-mail to Amy Edelstein of EnlightenNext, Mr. Levy stated that "if the allegations are to be found untrue we are of course to drop the article."

In the spirit of cooperation, my clients have answered the questions you posed, and the answers are enclosed. As you will see, it is the case that "the allegations are…untrue." I trust, and on behalf of my clients, request, that the article therefore be "dropped" in accordance with your message.

Please be advised that harm may come to my clients as a result of the proposed article. EnlightenNext is a nonprofit organization dedicated to aiding the spiritual development of interested persons. It is largely dependent on donations from the public to support its staff, as well as its retreats, seminars, publications, and speaking tours. False accusations published about it will have the foreseeable effect of unjustly diminishing its reputation and goodwill among the public that it seeks to contact and on which it is dependent for its support.

It appears that under Israeli law, an internet site may be liable for a defamatory publication even if it is not the direct editor of the material. See Boshmitz v. Aronowitz, No. C032986/03 (Magis. Ct. Tel Aviv). Here, NRG-Ma'ariv Online News is the direct editor and publisher, so Boshmitz is an a fortiori case.

It also may be the case that you may be subject to the personal jurisdiction of American courts. Among other factors, the article would be directed at my clients specifically and you have had contacts in the United States relative to them.

Thank you for your attention to this matter. Please contact me if you have any questions.

Sincerely yours,

Barry A. Fisher

Encl.

15

CONNECTING THE DOTS

I N his "Declaration of Integrity,"[60] Andrew Cohen writes: "You can take any particular incident out of context, as my detractors have made an art form of doing, and of course it creates a confusing impression…. One thing that has never failed to mystify me is that some people just don't connect the dots: If I really were the sadistic, irrational megalomaniac that I have been portrayed as, why in God's name would anybody stick around for ten or more years before finally 'waking up'?" (By "waking up" Cohen here means not liberation but something on the order of recognizing that he is a fraud.)

This is, I believe, a fair question, the answer to which is for the reader to decide. Though I have done everything in my power to address it in a way that is faithful to my own experience, the events I have described in this book remain, it would seem, open to interpretation. Thus, at the end as at the beginning, there seem to be two distinctly different "realities" to be considered, each with its own unique set of implications, or "dots to connect."

Let us first consider the perspective advanced by Andrew Cohen, according to which he is a realized master whose transmission of an authentic, absolute, impersonal "evolutionary impulse" is the overarching "higher context" for his role and conduct as a genuine and legitimate spiritual authority figure. The most relevant implication of this view is that, along with the contributors to this book and numerous other of his former followers, I am a deluded individual who, because I proved unable or unwilling to face my imperfect reflection in the glorious light of "the Absolute," have compulsively turned my back on "the Highest." Fair enough. Certainly in the arc of my career as Andrew's student I have considered this possibility more times than I can count (not exactly a recipe for "liberation"!) and was often convinced that he must be right. And now, as part of a continuing strategy for hiding my "failure" from myself, I have produced a self-serving book that falsely denounces one of the great religious luminaries of our era—whereas the *real* truth about Andrew Cohen ("for those who have eyes to see")[61] is that he is an Enlightened Being full of redemptory blessings for the world; his "revolution" is authentic; and those students humble enough to have remained with him through thick and thin are fulfilled, living expressions of unfolding human potential "at the leading edge."

I am not suggesting that this is a view to be easily or casually dismissed. As I have indicated elsewhere in this book, it is my own experience that Andrew Cohen presents a vast and credible perspective on human existence that is exciting, enlivening and inspiring, and that he produces an energetic transmission that moves people to connect or re-engage with the spiritual path. Further, his persuasively presented personal story seems to substantiate his claims. Many of Cohen's students, myself included, have been inspired to believe in his autobiography and to accept and defend his interpretation of its broad outlines: He was a dedicated seeker from an early age, had a spontaneous awakening experience that presaged his ultimate realization at thirty, was possessed of a rare purity of motivation that, at the time of his "final realization" and "perfect surrender" to his guru, helped to catalyze a total transformation that made it impossible thereafter for him to act out of ignorance such as to cause suffering to himself or others. At his teacher's request, he selflessly accepted as his mantle and destiny the responsibility of creating "a revolution among the young."[62] These claims are advanced in several of Cohen's self-published books, and enough of his followers believe them that anyone so predisposed could easily feel comfortable doing the same.

At the same time, though, it seems to me that any attempt to "connect the dots" should also take into account numerous

61 "The Teacher-Student Relationship: Genpo Roshi & Andrew Cohen," youtube.com, posted June 29, 2009
62 Cohen, Andrew, *My Master Is Myself: The Birth of a Spiritual Teacher* (second edition), Lenox, MA: What Is Enlightenment? Press, 1995, p. 61

examples of abuse on Cohen's part that, in many cases, require greater "artfulness" for him to justify than for me to remove from their "proper context." To give one of many possible examples: Do those students who, following Cohen's orders, lured a fellow student to a basement room at Foxhollow and each poured a bucket of paint over her head[63] really imagine that their guru is above ordinary spite, vindictiveness or malice, or is incapable of causing suffering?

What, then, does such an act signify?

Cohen insists that "if you were made aware of the enormous amount of time, care, attention, and support that had been given to the individual; understood the complex psychological/spiritual dynamics at work; saw it in the context of a collective endeavor to create a higher ideal for the noblest of reasons; and didn't conveniently forget that it was a freely chosen path; what may have appeared unreasonable often starts to look very different."[64] But to the extent that such incidents raise legitimate questions about Andrew Cohen's understanding of his own "attainment," their implications are at least as significant as those that follow from accepting at face value the version that he and his devotees would prefer the world to accept.

The most fundamental of these implications is that Cohen's interpretation of the defining events and experiences of his own life is a comprehensive myth that weaves together elements of truth and wishful thinking. And if Andrew Cohen believes some things about himself that are not true, then we are confronted, by definition, with the possibility that *he* is deluded. (God forbid that I should make something that sounds like a judgment about my former teacher!) Of course, many human beings are deluded to some extent, but some delusions are more harmful than others. Not to put too fine a point on it, the propagation of a glorious myth of personal sanctification and liberation, and the willingness of many others to accept it, is one definition of a potentially destructive cult.

---

63 See *Chapter 3.*
64 "A Declaration of Integrity," andrewcohen.org/blog, posted October 18, 2006

While we may be inspired by such myths, organizing our lives around them is not necessarily advisable, and doing so has implications for the followers as well as for the leader. In a recent dialogue with Dennis Genpo Merzel Roshi, Cohen described his attitude toward his students as follows: "[My] love for them is not for them as an individual but for them as a potential vessel for that which is higher. That's very hard for the ego to take, but from a certain point of view we could say it's not possible to love anyone more than that, because you love them so much that you actually don't care about their ego at all."[65] Yet to the extent that this explanation of Cohen's "teaching function" represents an unconscious rationalization for his manipulation of others in the service of a delusional myth, followers put themselves at considerable psychic risk by subjugating themselves to a "spiritual authority" who may actually be quite limited in his capacity for genuine love and compassion—and who may, in addition, feel an underlying contempt for them because of what they allow him to get away with at their own expense.

During the thirteen years of my career as a student, when I could be said to have been fully indoctrinated—to have "swallowed the myth," hook, line and sinker—I did not always do what I thought was right, but (like the members of the paint-bucket brigade) what seemed necessary to survive and thrive in a highly unconventional environment. To the extent that this characterization of my own experience is honest rather than merely "cynical," the situation of Cohen's current generation of devoted followers is unlikely to be much different. They, too, have given over their lives for the sake of an idealism predicated on what they may only later come to realize was a well-concealed lie. In some cases, their egos are stroked and gratified by their allotted roles, as mine was; and while they may fervently believe that they are doing good, the underlying hypocrisy of the situation as a whole ends up contributing, in the guise of Andrew Cohen's version of "goodness," to so much of what is already wrong with the world.

---

65 "The Teacher-Student Relationship: Genpo Roshi & Andrew Cohen," youtube.com, posted June 29, 2009

If this is so, it may be that the public work of a number of individuals associated with EnlightenNext is similarly compromised. Examples include Craig Hamilton, a newly self-proclaimed "pioneer in the emerging field of evolutionary spirituality" who, having "lived and worked in a dynamic living 'laboratory of evolution' under the direct guidance of EnlightenNext founder and spiritual teacher Andrew Cohen," and having played "a key role in the leadership of this thriving international spiritual community," looks back on the results as "extraordinary"[66]; Elizabeth Debold, a Harvard-trained developmental psychologist who is now (in her supposedly unbiased position as Senior Editor of Cohen's *EnlightenNext* magazine) trying to create objective measures of "higher development" designed to substantiate her "hypothesis" that people who take Cohen's retreats will display such traits[67]; Linus Roache, an internationally renowned actor, who directs EnlightenNext's New York center; Dave Gold and Michael Wombacher, authors of recent books selectively extolling their teacher, Andrew Cohen; Amy Edelstein, a member of EnlightenNext's Board of Directors, who has lied extensively to a journalist on Cohen's behalf;[68]and Carter Phipps, the current Executive Editor of *EnlightenNext* magazine, whose reprinted article on the Huffington Post ("What Ever Happened to Truth?") takes others to task for the sort of revisionist dishonesty and abuse of power he seems perfectly willing to overlook in his teacher and Editor-in-chief.[69]

And what of Cohen's celebrity endorsers—Genpo Roshi, Ken Wilber, Rupert Sheldrake, Deepak Chopra, Bernie Glassman, to name only a few—who offer their implicit support by agreeing to participate in his forums? To what extent have they considered the

66 craighamilton.us; integralenlightenment.com
67 "What is 'Higher Development'?", posted June 12, 2009 (US archive), enlightennext.org/webcast
68 See *Chapter 14*, Yonatan Levy's "interview" with EnlightenNext.
69 "[It] seems to be more important these days," laments Phipps, "that we are tolerant of divergent opinions than that we judge those opinions as true or false based on their merits. The reason tolerance has more intellectual cachet and judgment is largely because we have lost confidence in our capacity to ascertain truth. We have seen how 'truth' is so often, well...not true. We have witnessed how easily it can be manipulated by the powerful..." (huffingtonpost.com/carter-phipps/whatever-happened-to-trut_b_191925.html)

possibility that the extensive allegations against Cohen exist for valid reasons — that where there is smoke there is every likelihood of fire? Are they poor judges of character? Are they as vulnerable to Cohen's manipulations as anyone else? Are they swayed by Cohen's humble-seeming profession of the Bodhisattva vow "to enlighten the world"?[70] Or are they taking advantage of the strategic media opportunity that Andrew Cohen represents with no thought for the possible consequences? Does Genpo Roshi, for example, make any practical distinction — particularly with respect to the risk of abuse — between surrendering unconditionally to a manipulative cult leader and submitting to the guidance of a sanctioned teacher within the framework of an established tradition? Why not? However accurate it may be, Cohen's maverick reputation for questionable conduct is certainly no secret.

Further, what are the implications of these "high-level" interactions between "spiritual authorities" such as Cohen and Wilber for our understanding of spiritual life as a whole? Is there validity, for example, in Cohen's notions of "verticality" and "hierarchy," or in his (and Wilber's) use of the Spiral Dynamics conceptual model as a means of dismissing critics by characterizing their legitimate concerns as "narcissistic" postmodern expressions of "lower" developmental levels? Are these hierarchical principles applicable to followers in all situations, regardless of the behavior of the self-appointed spiritual authority figures that demand their "surrender" as a necessary precondition for the transcendence of egoic self-delusion? If not, why haven't the reservations of these respected figures (assuming they have any) been publicly articulated?

Recent EnlightenNext webcasts have stressed the importance of the second of Wilber's "Three Faces of God," i.e., the living manifestation of the divine in the form of the guru before whom the devotee must prostrate, as Cohen puts it, "on bended knee." On one such webcast, Terry Patten, a former follower of the recently deceased American guru/cult-leader Adi Da (a.k.a. Da

---

70 "The Teacher-Student Relationship: Genpo Roshi & Andrew Cohen," youtube.com, posted June 29, 2009

Free John)—whose "corruption" and "megalomania" Cohen him-self once pointedly criticized[71]—was interviewed enthusiastically by two of Cohen's students, Elizabeth Debold and Jeff Carreira.[72] Patten, a Wilber co-author who offers international workshops explaining the "The Three Faces of God," complimented Cohen's student body as a whole for its ready receptivity to the notion of surrender to the guru—neglecting, like Genpo Roshi, to acknowl-edge both the many instances in which "surrender" has turned out to be a code-word for misguided loyalty and the obvious dan-gers of surrendering to a "megalomaniac" whoever he (or she) might be. Perhaps not surprisingly, Debold and Carreira, good disciples that they are, didn't raise these issues either.[73]

Adi Da's explanation of "Second Face of God" devotional practice, transcribed from a video on youtube.com,[74] reads thus:

> Having no rug to stand on, no separateness to define you in separa-tion from me, surrendered in the perfect sense so that you are tacitly directly in the room with me, the room of my indivisible person, with your shoes at the door—in other words having stepped into the space of indivisibility—that's the perfect practice of devotion to me. If you don't know me enough to know that's the only right relation-ship to me then you don't recognize me, you're not feeling my actual state. Mistaking me for somebody else, for somebody like yourself, you're seeing in me your own reflection in some sense; you're being a narcissist when you're looking at me. So without recognition of

71 See, for example, "Holy Madness: The Dangerous and Disillusioning Example of Da Free John" (Introduction), *What Is Enlightenment?* magazine, v. 9, Spring/Summer, 1996
72 "The Second Face of God," posted May 29, 2009 (US archive), enlightennext.org/webcast
73 Long gone, apparently, are the days of Cohen's emphasis on "the need for clear ex-amples," when his insistence on strict correspondence between "word and deed" in those assuming the role of spiritual teacher alienated him from so many of his colleagues in what he referred to, at that time, as "the modern spiritual world." More recently, he has found it advantageous to form public alliances with such figures, and to articulate his studied assessments of their shortcomings only in private. Adi Da, once an early object of Cohen's justifiable criticism (for, among other things, his sexual and pharmaceutical excesses), now, as a fellow advocate of a hierarchical doctrine that Cohen evidently finds more convenient than the ethical challenges of leading by example, appears to be a rehabil-itated figure in the EnlightenNext pantheon. (This may be no coincidence, as Cohen's ally Wilber is, like Patten, a former Da devotee.) It is certainly noteworthy that in contrast to Cohen's insistence, earlier in his career, on the importance of publicizing the flaws of other spiritual teachers (see, for example, "A Crisis of Trust," enlightennext.org/magazine/j9/andrew_crisis.asp), he now seeks vigorously to combat attempts to publicize his own.
74 "Adi Da Samraj—Beyond the Familiar," youtube.com, posted June 23, 2008

me, and true turning to me, true devotion to me, you're actually seeing yourself, a projection of yourself, a superimposition of your own limitations on my form.

And asked by the journalist John Horgan to explain his assertion that his students should *never leave him,* Andrew Cohen offers this equally striking rationale for total, uncritical surrender: "Let's say the Buddha was alive today. Let's say someone that great, that enlightened, that pure, that perfect, with such a great teaching, was still alive. I mean, could someone be too attached to someone like that? The more attached you get to a person like that, the more free, literally, you become" —adding, however, that "anybody who wants to be free is going to have to bend his knee.... However that happens, it doesn't really matter, as long as it happens."[75]

Is it any wonder, then, that in Cohen's community, "leaving" and "failure" are considered to be virtually synonymous, and that students tend to live in greater fear of giving in to the impulse to escape his control than of enduring the familiar compromises and discomforts of soldiering on? "As harsh as it may sound to some," Cohen writes, "the simple truth is that my most virulent critics are almost all former students who failed miserably."[76] What exactly is the nature of Cohen's power over his devotees that they are willing not only to endure his abuses for extended periods but also to ignore or rationalize his behavior, and to lie to the public on his behalf when called upon to do so? Only a large group of people who have been uniformly indoctrinated could collectively believe—as they do about former members like myself—that we are all, consistently and almost without exception, "miserable failures." Is it possible that there is some mass form of Stockholm Syndrome being lived out at Foxhollow and EnlightenNext's centers around the world? If so, how does this authoritarian dynamic relate to the broader "revolution in consciousness and culture" that is the goal of EnlightenNext's feverish public outreach? Is Cohen's "revolution" authentically spiritual and cultural, or is it

75 Horgan, John, "The Myth of the Totally Enlightened Guru," www.johnhorgan.org/work27.htm
76 "A Declaration of Integrity," andrewcohen.org/blog, posted October 18, 2006

rather political—in the sense that the motivation underlying political rhetoric, when it is not the propagation of truth, is often the desire to convince, cajole, manipulate, hierarchize, dominate and humiliate?

One discovers, then, as a counterpoint to Cohen's dismissive assessment of the motives and failures of his critics, that "connecting the dots" leads to an equally viable (and far more disturbing) conclusion: that EnlightenNext's web of publications, centers, student groups, enlisted experts and strategic alliances comprises a sizeable myth-based social complex fueled—at this point principally via the internet—by a powerful mixture of genuine insight and disingenuous propaganda; and that it can be as true of a spiritual community as of the larger society it seeks to transform that the appeal of its prevailing ideology guarantees neither the wholesomeness of its underlying motivations nor the integrity of its leaders. As Erich Fromm pointed out a little over half a century ago,

> It is naïvely assumed that the fact that [a] majority of people share certain ideas or feelings proves the validity of these ideas and feelings. Nothing is further from the truth.... Just as there is a 'folie à deux' there is a 'folie à millions.' The fact that millions of people share the same vices does not make these vices virtues, the fact that they share so many errors does not make the errors to be truths, and the fact that millions of people share the same form of mental pathology does not make these people sane.[77]

And as Andrew Cohen himself observed in a concise and prescient early teaching dialogue that deserves to be read in its entirety,

> The minute anybody allows themselves to tolerate corruption they become a part of it. These people desperately don't want to see the depth of the corruption that they themselves are immersed in. The security of their spiritual well-being *depends* on the fact that no matter what, the actions of the guru are *never* questioned. Because their hearts are so invested in the guru, they will make almost any rationalization or justification for the guru's actions. They will do almost anything in order to protect that love that the guru has revealed to them.

---

77 Fromm, Erich, *The Sane Society*, London: Routledge, 1955, pp.14-15

This is spiritual slavery and prostitution of the soul. In weak-minded people the seal of enlightenment becomes a license for abuse.[78]

The lessons of the EnlightenNext story have yet to be learned in their entirety, and I share with all of Andrew Cohen's students the hope that its unfolding will be of benefit to the many idealistic participants whose time and energy it consumes, along with the precautionary warnings that my experience tells me those who live it are going to need. Ultimately, however, I do not believe it serves any useful purpose to sugarcoat the "facts on the ground" in the interest of evenhandedness. Though I wish neither ill nor harm to Cohen's current followers, it is my informed and considered opinion that membership in his community represents an invitation to waste one's time and energy, and possibly one's entire life, in the service of a destructive and damaging myth, as well as a dubious opportunity to entangle oneself ever more deeply and dangerously in its creator's elaborately constructed lies. Those of us who have left the EnlightenNext community did so for what have turned out to be compellingly good reasons: No "teacher" worthy of the name would subject his students to the kinds of mental, physical and financial abuses described in this book, and no "spiritual leader" who requires his followers to internalize and reinforce a fantasy of his own perfection deserves a platform for his hypocritical ideology of "evolutionary enlightenment."

In 1996, Andrew Cohen wrote,

> ...I feel it is so essential that those individuals, who have been fortunate enough to have fallen into the miracle of transcendent spiritual realization, be able to demonstrate an attainment that clearly and unambiguously expresses the evolutionary potential of the race. For as long as this demand is not made, and those who are showing the way for others are allowed to demonstrate the very same schizophrenic condition of contradictory impulses as everyone else, then the attain-

78 "Spiritual Slavery and Prostitution of the Soul," *What Is Enlightenment?* magazine, v. 9, Spring/Summer 1996 (online: enlightennext.org/magazine/j9/andrew_slavery.asp)

ment of true simplicity and unequivocal victory over ignorance will remain a myth.[79]

I applaud Cohen's good intentions, which I trusted enough to offer him thirteen years of my life. Unfortunately, though the "teaching" he has cobbled together contains elements of perennial wisdom, time has revealed that it rests on a foundation of dishonesty, corruption and pernicious abuse of power that undermines whatever positive effects it might otherwise have produced. Knowing what I know, if I were a parent whose children had elected to join Cohen's community, I would be fearful, upset and deeply concerned for their welfare, and resentful of the carelessness with which respected spiritual authorities advance Cohen's "mission" by endorsing it without any consideration for the abuses they may thereby be facilitating. Without realizing it, those who support Andrew Cohen from a safe distance—or worse, sanction his abuses—increase the potential of harm to the followers they help him to attract or retain. In the end, it is my concern for the individuals involved at the many levels of the EnlightenNext network—past, present and future—that has inspired me to undertake and complete this project. Whether or not they feel they need it, I wish healing for them all.

79 Cohen, Andrew, *An Unconditional Relationship to Life: The Odyssey of an American Spiritual Teacher*, Lenox, MA: What Is Enlightenment? Press, 1995, p. 47 (online: "A Crisis of Trust,"enlightennext.org/magazine/j9/andrew_crisis.asp)

BIBLIOGRAPHY

Armstrong, Karen. *The Spiral Staircase: My Climb Out of Darkness,* New York: Anchor Books, 2004

Batchelor, Stephen. *Buddhism Without Beliefs: A Contemporary Guide to Awakening,* New York: Riverhead, 1997

_____. *Living With the Devil: A Meditation on Good and Evil,* New York: Riverhead, 2004

Berry, Thomas. *The Great Work: Our Way into the Future,* New York: Three Rivers Press, 2000

Chodron, Pema. *When Things Fall Apart: Heart Advice for Difficult Times,* Boston: Shambala, 1997

Diamond, Jared. *Collapse: How Societies Choose to Fail or Succeed,* New York: Viking, 2005

Faulk, Jeffrey. *Stripping the Gurus,* Toronto: Million Monkey Press, 2009

Harris, Sam. *The End of Faith: Religion, Terror and the Future of Reason,* New York: W.W. Norton, 2005

James, William. *The Varieties of Religious Experience,* Mineola, NY: Dover Publications, 2002

Jensen, Derrick. *A Language Older than Words,* White River Junction, VT: Chelsea Green, 2004

Krakauer, Jon. *Under the Banner of Heaven: A Story of Violent Faith,* New York: Anchor Books, 2004

Kramer, Joel and Alstad, Diana. *The Guru Papers: Masks of Authoritarian Power,* Berkeley: Frog Books, 1993

Krishnamurti, J. *Freedom From the Known,* New York: HarperCollins, 1975

Maharaj, Nisargadatta. *I Am That: Talks with Sri Nisargadatta Maharaj.* Durham, NC: Acorn Press, 1990

Mandela, Nelson. *Long Walk to Freedom: The Autobiography of Nelson Mandela,* Boston: Little Brown, 1994

McKenna, Jed. *Spiritually Incorrect Enlightenment,* Iowa City, IA: Wisefool Press, 2004

Milgram, Stanley. *Obedience to Authority,* New York: Harper Perennial, 2004

Oakes, Len. *Prophetic Charisma: The Psychology of Revolutionary Religious Personalities,* Syracuse, NY: Syracuse University Press, 1997

Peck, M. Scott. *People of the Lie,* New York: Touchstone, 1985

Poonja, H.W.L. *The Truth Is.* York Beach, ME: Red Wheel/Weiser, 2000

Rumi, Jalal al-Din. *The Essential Rumi,* San Francisco: HarperOne, 1997

Sherrill, Martha. *The Buddha From Brooklyn,* New York: Random House, 2000

Storr, Anthony. *Feet of Clay,* New York: Free Press, 1997

Tarlo, Luna. *The Mother of God,* New York: Plover/Autonomedia, 1997

Tolle, Eckhart. *The Power of Now: A Guide to Spiritual Enlightenment,* San Francisco: New World Library, 2004

Tutu, Desmond. *No Future Without Forgiveness,* New York: Image, 2000

Van der Braak, Andre. *Enlightenment Blues: My Years with an American Guru,* Rhinebeck, NY: Monkfish, 2003

CONTRIBUTORS

Since leaving Andrew Cohen's community over ten years ago, **Wendyl Smith** has been involved in micro-enterprise development both in the United States and, for the last eight years, in Bali. Actively engaged in Buddhist and Taoist practices, she lives in a mountain village on the edge of an ancient caldera. Her life has brought her into daily communion with many creative, kind and generous people — an extraordinary merging of international and local cultures and innovation.

Karen Merigo moved to the United States from Italy in the late 1980s to live in Andrew Cohen's community. She was a senior student from 1988 to 1996. Upon leaving, she decided to stay in California with her good friends. She now lives in San Francisco, working at an art school and learning to follow her bliss.

Susan Bridle was a student of Andrew Cohen from 1992 until 2003, and was an editor of his magazine, *What is Enlightenment?* (now known as *EnlightenNext*), during that time. She is now completing her Ph.D. at the University of Denver's Graduate School of International Studies in the fields of international political economy, international relations, and political theory. She teaches at the University of Colorado at Denver, and has been practicing Zen Buddhism since 2002 under the guidance of Henry Danan, Roshi, at the Zen Center of Denver. She lives with her partner, Brian, in Lakewood, Colorado.

Richard Pitt spent eight years in the spiritual community of Andrew Cohen. Since leaving in 1995, he has lived in San Francisco, practicing homeopathic medicine and running a homeopathic school. In early 2009, he took a four-month sabbatical in India, mostly in Tiruvannamalai, home of the famous Indian saint Ramana Maharshi.

Mario Puljiz fled the violence of the Balkans where he was born, moving to the United Kingdom in 1991. There he pursued his interest in spiritual matters, which led him to Andrew Cohen in 1994. After joining Cohen's community he met Caroline Franklyn, who, like him, had left her homeland under life-threatening circumstances. Mario's chapter is testimony to his affection and respect for his friend, who died in 1999. Mario left the community shortly afterwards in 2000, and has since been running a real estate business in London.

Luna Tarlo is the author of *The Mother of God,* a memoir about the three-and-a-half years she spent as a disciple of her son, Andrew Cohen. She has always been a writer and continues to write now. Her most recent publication is the novel *Eilat,* published by Rain Mountain Press.

RESOURCES

American Guru website: americanguru.net

WhatEnlightenment??! blog: whatenlightenment.net

Dr. Arthur J. Deikman: deikman.com

LaVergne, TN USA
08 October 2009
160308LV00001B/109/P